The Other Side
of ANGER

A Son's Search for Peace

Jack Perry, Jr.

The Other Side of Anger
A Son's Search for Peace

Copyright © 2019 by Jack Perry, Jr.

Jack Perry, Jr., Source Point Coaching
https://sourcepointcoaching.com

Interior and Cover design by Mark E. Anderson
www.AquaZebra.com

 AquaZebra™
Book Publishing

www.AquaZebra.com
Web, Book & Print Design
Cathedral City, CA

For information about special discounts for bulk purchases or to book Jack Perry, Jr. for a speaking engagement or training event please contact Source Point Coaching at (770) 330-9212 or jackperry@sourcepointcoaching.com

ISBN: 978-0-9905827-0-0

ISBN lists AquaZebra as the publisher

Library of Congress Control Number: 2014945856

Printed in the United States of America

First Edition
Second Printing, March 2019

Dedication

To My Wonderful Mother, Annette,
and my sisters, Beverley and Toni. I love you.

Acknowledgments

I would like to thank Tracy Cleary for her love and support and encouraging me to get it all out there. And I would like to thank all of those wonderful people who have crossed my path in life for making it a rich and growing experience.

—Jack Perry

Table of Contents

Introduction

I had to write this book. My heart told me I couldn't walk away from this book or its subject matter. I'm not a writer, I'm not a highly-educated thinker—I'm just Jack. I am a son, who truly didn't understand his father until the end. I decided to write about a subject that most communities, churches, families, and organizations sweep under the rug: domestic violence. But domestic violence is rampant in our society. It remains well hidden until the straw breaks the camel's back and someone is shot, killed, or seriously injured in that final moment of rage. So many women have quietly shared their story with me, begging that it go no further out of fear of reprisal from an angry husband, boss, son, or partner. I have witnessed domestic violence and I have been a victim of domestic violence. I have been an angry man and I have witnessed the pain angry men can cause, both at work and at home.

This book is about awareness for both men and women; it is not meant to bash men. On the contrary, I write this book to help all those who may recognize themselves in these pages. It's written out of love and respect for humanity. For all those whom I may have hurt on my journey in life, I deeply apologize. And for those who have hurt me, I truly do forgive you.

—Jack

The Other Side of ANGER

A Son's Search for Peace

Jack Perry, Jr.

Chapter 1

My Childhood

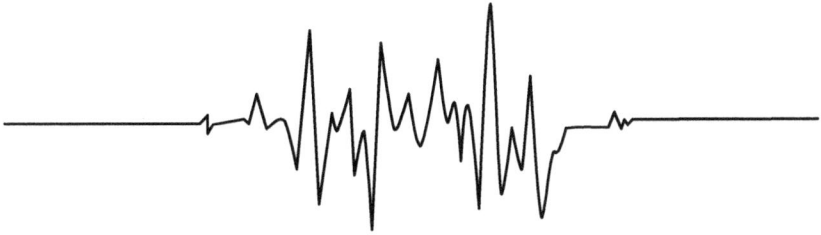

I don't remember ever being happy as a child. I only remember turmoil, anger, or frustration. The atmosphere in our home was constantly tense—a strain resulting from my dad's yelling and arguing, always seeming to involve alcohol. I remember seeing my mother abused. I remember seeing my father yell and scream at her until she cowered like a little child. I remember seeing my father hit my mother. I didn't quite understand it as a little boy. I knew there was something not quite right with that behavior, but I didn't know what it was. I just knew it was wrong and it stirred a deep, strong emotion in me.

One of the things I learned early on is that kids see everything: every change in mood, every behavior, every decision, every action. Even when you think a child is not watching you, he or she sees and hears everything. Their minds are constantly deciding what is real, what is right, what is logical, what is helpful or hurtful to others. As a little boy, I might have been playing with a toy or concentrating on some small task, and I'd hear my dad speak ill of other people or about what was on the news or about somebody he had just finished speaking to on the phone. It left me with a confused impression of the world. My father would be nice, kind, and polite while talking to a person one minute, and then immediately switch to negative talk when the person's back was turned. It didn't add up. I was left feeling unsettled about this for many years.

My father was always angry and raging at something in his life. When I spoke to my father, I never knew how he would react. When I thought things were going well, it could just take a small trigger—a change in the weather, a news report on the television, maybe someone cut him off in traffic, or he was having a bad day at work—and his whole attitude would instantly change. Everyone present would be affected.

I remember anxiously waiting every day for my father to come home. "Your dad's coming home," my mom would say. "Go to your rooms." No one could predict his mood when he walked in the front door. Life in our home was never predictable.

Unfortunately, as a young boy, I accepted that type of behavior as normal. I had nothing else to compare it to. That's how men are, I thought. Hitting your wife or being verbally abusive to women and other people seemed normal, too. Fortunately, as I grew up, I was introduced to positive role models through Boy Scouts, football, and my schoolteachers. Through them, I realized the abuse of other people is not normal behavior, and I was able to change that paradigm and beliefs about myself. I decided to make better choices about how I viewed my own relationships, my friends, and my marriage—but more on that later.

I grew up in a military family. We traveled a lot and saw many different beautiful and wonderful places: Scotland, England, Goose Bay (Newfoundland), North Dakota, and Tucson, Arizona. As a child, I learned that it was necessary and, on the surface, not so difficult to say goodbye to people. It wasn't hard to integrate into other families and other military bases and other schools, though it could be stressful.

In my family, as with many other families that endure domestic violence, you were told to never, ever talk outside your home about personal family matters. Never talk about what goes on inside your home. Never talk about things that are upsetting. Never talk about the bad things that happen, because home life is supposed to be perfect. It was a façade. My home, where I grew up as a young boy, was sad. The days were marred with anger, fear, and unpredictability. On the outside, we may have looked like the perfect family. But on the inside, there was a lot of turmoil—all due to the inner unhappiness of one person.

I remember looking at other families and wondering how they seemed so "put together." They were always smiling and happy and energetic around other people. They had interesting conversations, and they were free to tell all. I just didn't quite understand it. In our home, we were always on pins and needles, never knowing when our angry dad was going to show up. Everybody else around us seemed to be so perfect. Was that real or perceived? I'll never know. But, I did know our family was not as we presented ourselves to the world.

Christmas always seemed to be a time of celebration and happiness for most other people, but, as a child, I didn't like Christmas. I remember one year, on the military base in England, being very excited as we drove up to a lot where they were selling Christmas trees. I got out of the car and ran toward the trees, but my father yelled at me because I was acting like the small, eight-year-old boy I was. He pulled a switch off one of the Christmas trees and hit me with it on my left arm, leaving welts and causing my arm to go numb. I was so excited to be choosing a tree, and I couldn't understand why he was so angry with me. I was angry, too—and bewildered and confused. But I could never ask him about it, out of fear.

I remember that smell—that evergreen smell, that distinctive Christmas tree smell. It's amazing what a child remembers. And even today, when I smell that pine smell, I regress back to that beating in my childhood, the beating of an eight-year-old boy. I'm sure that, every Christmas of my life, that vivid memory will creep back into my mind.

As a child, I didn't like sports—and it's not because I

wasn't good at them. I didn't like team play because my father took the joy out of the game. His anger would come out at any opportunity. If I wasn't good enough or didn't make a basket, he would stand on the sidelines and yell at me. He would scream, "You're not good enough!" He would rant and bellow, "You're worthless! What are you doing out there? Get off the court!" And if I made a basket, instead of celebrating, he would stick it in other peoples' faces. "Yeah, there you go," he would gloat. "See what he's doing?" I absolutely hated it. Every year, I would try out for various sports, but in the back of my mind I knew: *If I make this team, my father will be on the sidelines yelling at me and telling me I'm not good enough.*

My father told me to always fight for what I want. Take the ball. Be aggressive. Knock the other guy down if you have to. Once, I was playing basketball on a military base in Canada and I was angry because my father was yelling at me from the sidelines. So, instead of just playing by the rules, I grabbed the ball and fought the guy who was holding it. I knocked him down, and then I thought: *Good. Now my dad's going to be happy because I fought this guy.* Instead, the referee kicked me out of the game. My dad still got mad. I was confused, frustrated, and deflated. I didn't know which way to turn. That was my role model as a small boy, as a young man. It made no sense at all.

I also hated report cards. The end of term was a very tense and angry time in our lives. I'd come home with my report card in hand, and if I got a C, it was like the sky was falling. My mother would be upset because she was the one who'd have to deal with my dad's yelling and screaming for the next couple of days. He'd yell that we kids were worthless, that we weren't able to do anything, and that we wouldn't accomplish anything.

My mother would always say to us, "You'd better go upstairs," or, "Go to your room and wait for your father to get home because he's going to be very upset." I hated report card days. I absolutely hated them. I'd sit in my room, waiting. When my dad saw my grades, he just looked at me. He already had an electrical cord from a lamp in his hand. And he proceeded to hit me with it—on my legs and my back; he left welts on my body. It stung and it hurt and it left an imprint in my mind that report cards were bad. No matter how good my grades were, report cards were bad. And it was a way for my dad to release his energy and his anger on us. He wanted us to meet his perceived bar of excellence. And when we failed, we failed him and his expectations. As a boy, I didn't know what to do, where to turn, or who to talk to. So I learned to stuff it down and look for an escape, a way out of this shame and confusion.

As an adult, many years later, my mother confided in me that she had told my dad, "If he goes to school or to the hospital, or if the police see those cuts and bruises on his back and his legs, you're going to go to jail." But as I said earlier, nothing negative ever left our house. It was all behind closed doors.

One time, my dad was waiting for me to come back from the movies. I remember walking through the woods close to my home; I was especially happy. I had seen the great movie *Oliver!* by director Carol Reed. My dad was standing out in the driveway washing the car. Life was good; heck, I was only twelve years old. I was in a good mood. It was a fun movie. I was very uplifted, very spiritually connected at the moment; it was one of those happy moments in my life—until I saw my dad.

He was wearing a green shirt and tan pants; I can see it as vividly today as I did decades ago. I tried to walk past him and he asked me: "Where were you?" He blocked me. "Why are you late?" I looked at my watch. I was only ten or fifteen minutes late. I told him I was taking my time getting home; I didn't know I was late. I started to walk past him. *Wham!* I felt a crash against the back of my head. He had violently slapped me with his hand, almost knocking me over. That was his way of telling me, "Don't be late again!" Lesson learned. Message received. I was so confused: happy one moment—stunned, humiliated, and ashamed the next.

I never had any real conversations with my father like those father-and-son talks you see on TV. My sisters, my mom, and I watched *Eight Is Enough*, where Dick Van Patten played the father. We use to watch it in private when my dad wasn't around. I remember my father would see that show on TV, scoff and say, "That's not real. Families aren't like that." It wasn't until later in my life that I realized that my father really didn't know what a family was supposed to be like. He was just an angry, bitter man. He only knew one way to rule, and that was through serious wrath. That TV make-believe wasn't part of our reality, and especially not his.

As a child, I wanted to get out of where I was. I was always conjuring up ways to escape. I even thought of running away. But being on a military base, isolated from the general population, made it very difficult. Being a military brat, you wouldn't get far—especially if you were stationed overseas and you were a young, black kid. You stood out. I felt stifled, fearful, uncertain, overwhelmed, and scared. I wanted something better. But I just decided to deal with it, like my mother. Do my time and wait for my break, when I turned that magic age of eighteen.

I have a distinct memory of being about eight or nine years old and living in England. My father had gone on a drinking binge and had abused my mother the night before, beating her. The next morning he got up and went to work as usual. And, as he often did, he called my mother to apologize (very typical behavior for an alcoholic and an abuser). "Gee, honey, I'm sorry," he would say. "I apologize," as if little had happened and it was over. My mother, being the beautiful woman that she is, would accept it and life would get back to normal for about a day or two. When I was eight years old—the same age as the picture on the back of this book—I remember my sisters and I cleaning my mother's blood off the carpet. In my little mind, this was life, and this was what normal looked like.

It wasn't until later, as an adult and looking back on my life, that I realized what a hero my mother was to me. I have strong memories of my mother always trying to keep it all together through all the madness and unpredictability. We've had a very special bond over the years; I will always love and fiercely protect her. I think it's because I saw her suffer so much—physically, mentally, and emotionally. I saw all the differences between what the rest of society was doing, what was right in the world, and what my dad was doing. As a young boy, I knew that what my dad was doing was wrong. I just did not know what to do about it. I was young and helpless. Because of that, I believe, I grew to love and cherish my mother's love and to be her protector in a much closer, deeper way. In spite of the fact that I couldn't protect her from my father's anger, I would protect her from the world.

Eventually, there was a time in my life—when I was about sixteen years old—that I realized my father couldn't manipulate or hurt me anymore. I stood up to him. I stood up to my father, finally. I think at that point he knew that his abuse of my mom was over. He had no more power. One evening, I heard him threaten my mother and I had an epiphany. It just clicked in me that what I saw in society and read in school, what I witnessed on TV and learned in church was right—and what was happening in my home was wrong. I told my dad, "Never, ever put your hands on my mother again." I stared him down. I wasn't going to back down. I owned that moment. I was ready to move out if he kicked me out of the house. I was prepared to have him arrested if necessary.

Sadly, as with most domestic violence situations, the abuse didn't end there. And my mother's fear was constant. She asked me, "What happens after you go, Jack? I have to deal with it when you're gone. Don't create problems."

I was once again between a rock and a hard place. My heart hurt.

Chapter 2

My Father's Anger

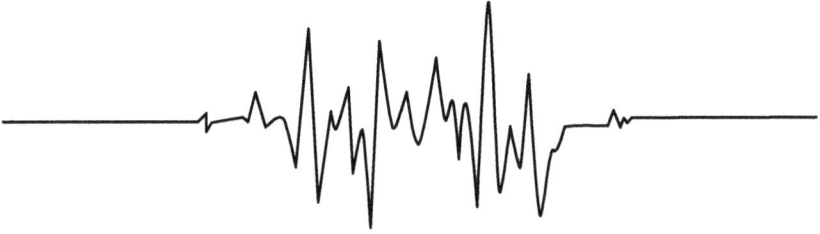

I never knew when my dad's anger was going to show up. Sometimes it happened at home when we were happy, when things were smooth and we were having a good time, maybe watching television. Or, sometimes, we would be coming home from school or having friends over to work on a school project when angry dad showed up. It didn't matter, because, as soon as my father walked into a room, the energy completely changed. You never knew what was going to happen next. But, you could be certain it wouldn't be pleasant.

My father talked often about physical violence. He used to reminisce about his time overseas in the military and people getting stabbed or shot. He always seemed to relish it. He seemed to be caught up in the scene and enjoying the description of the events. It was sickening.

The only way he made a point with anyone was by yelling.

He was loud. He was a screamer. We never understood his message. We only sensed his frustration and experienced his anger. We learned that a point made louder was not a valid point. We also learned, and it became common for us, when my father came home or showed up some place, to either change our demeanor or go hide. That's not a healthy way for a child to grow up. When you hear or see your father coming, and you have to change who you are just to survive, there's something very wrong. You feel bewildered, concerned, unaccepted, and unloved. When your mother has to feel fearful in her own home when her husband comes home, something is wrong. That's not the way to live in this one short, precious life that God has given us.

I remember my father talking *at* me instead of talking *to* me. It was as if he was the drill instructor and I was a private for him to belittle or put in my place. I don't ever remember having a good face-to-face, deep, and honest conversation with my dad. Not even the slightest exchange of empathy, love, kindness, or forgiveness. I didn't realize until later in my life how important it is for a young boy to have that connection with his dad. We lost so much with each other that we will never get back. Ever. And that's sad.

My father was very insulting. It wasn't until I was older that I realized this stemmed from his own insecurity. I remember he would insult my sisters—belittle them, make fun of them, tell them they were worthless and they wouldn't amount to anything. He dictated their schedules, which boys they could date, and their curfews. He'd also complain that he didn't like his work, didn't like his bosses, didn't like an assignment, and didn't like this-or-that. This person was too stupid. That person shouldn't be there. That person shouldn't have gotten promoted. "It should have been me," he would complain. "It should have been somebody else." In any event, at any time, he was always an angry man—always, always angry. I never once looked at my father with love, acceptance, and admiration, or as a role model.

He'd blame other people for things that didn't go right. "It was their fault," he would determine. "It wasn't my fault." It seemed to get worse after he drank. He seemed to drink to ease his pain. He'd come home in an angry mood, and, to relieve his unhappiness, he'd have something to drink. But instead of helping, it just made it worse. His anger increased. His emotions grew unstable, and everyone within range became a target. I used to hate to hear the sound of my father's feet walking across the floor. In his hand, he'd have a glass filled with alcohol, and I could hear the ice cubes jingling in the glass as he walked down the hallway. Sometimes I still hear it. You knew it was a sign that all hell was about to break loose. *Everybody, go to your corners, because the fight's on for the next several hours. Everyone run, hide; find protection and safety on your own.*

I lay in bed many nights listening to my mom and dad argue, hoping and praying that I wouldn't hear the crashing of glass or something being thrown—or worse. I prayed I wouldn't hear my mother being thrown up against the wall or being physically beaten. I prayed I wouldn't hear her scream and pleas for help and whispers of "Honey, please don't do that." It's a sad, sick way for a young boy, a young girl, or any family member to grow up. All because of anger—my father's *furious* anger. And it was directed at me and at each member of my family.

A parent's anger can, and will, breed anger in a child. When a child doesn't understand—that's not normal. When a young boy or girl sees that kind of anger in a father, that child starts to believe in that behavior. He or she believes that it's a normal way of life, that it's the logical way to act in all situations. When children grow up that way, it perpetuates a vicious, deadly cycle. When will that anger show up? What will cause it to emerge? Anger breeds anger, and it will affect many people and those who love them. It will affect everything. Everything.

Chapter 3

My Mother

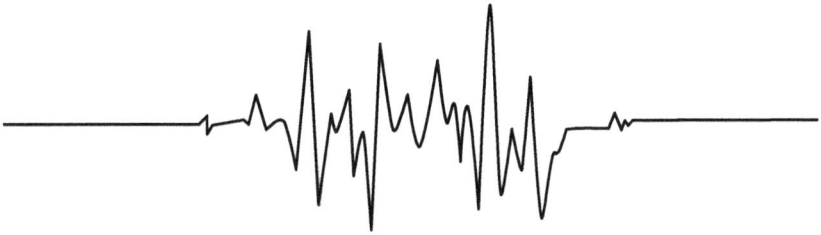

My mother is the glue that kept our family together. She is a beautiful and gracious woman, to this day. No matter how bad things were, she always had a smile. She always prayed to God and had a Bible close by. She was a good Christian, a good Catholic woman.

One day, my mother sat down with me and told me about how she met my father and why she married him. It was very illuminating. She had spent a good portion of her childhood in a convent to avoid sexual abuse. Understandably, after this upbringing, she was looking for freedom from that life. She met my father, and he was a handsome man. My dad said and did all the right things and won my mother's heart. She trusted him. But she had no idea what she was buying into. They married and moved back to the United States from England.

Relationships remind me of an iceberg. You see only see the top of it—the visible 10 percent. That's what shows up when you meet someone for the first time, when you shake their hand. You get their visible 10 percent, their basic first look, the tip of the iceberg. Their personality is what initially sells them. But as time goes on, you get to know that person better. When your back's against the wall, when you need the person the most, when you both go through trials and tribulations together, when you need a hug, when you need a friend, when you need to have a critical conversation—that's when you know true character, the person below the surface. That's the 90 percent of the iceberg you don't see—the part that is submerged, the inside of who he or she really is. True colors are revealed during stressful times, during life's many twists and turns; especially if you're married to that person. That's the part my mother didn't immediately see.

My mother was abused as a child. I didn't find that out until later in my life. It made sense to me, in a strange way. Possibly, in my mother's mind, when my father abused her, it was normal. But it's not. As a healthy adult, I know it's not. And I want to show and tell everyone—my mother included: It is NOT normal to be abused. It is not healthy and it is not acceptable.

No matter what happened, my mother protected us.

After my father went on a drinking binge he would have one of his anger episodes—tearing up the house, getting mad and raging at everybody. I remember many, many times sitting on the bed with my mother putting her arms around all of us, hoping that my father wasn't going to come in the room and hurt any of us. She sheltered us within her arms, having already endured his abuse, as a way of sparing us from our father's anger and wrath. What a sad way to grow up. What a sad way to live—all because of anger.

The saddest thing was that my mother lost herself. After fifty-six years of marriage to my father, she lost who she was and who she was meant to be on this earth. As many women often do in abusive relationships, she didn't see a way out. Many elect to stay and tolerate the abuse, frightened of threats or financial insecurity. I've learned through their stories that many women get to a place where they give of themselves for the family, for the child, for the husband, for everyone and to everyone, *except* themselves. Over time, they lose who they are as a person. They lose their passion, set aside their talents, and just exist. They lose sight of their purpose in life and what they want to contribute to the world.

If you're in an abusive relationship with somebody who is very angry, then who you are can be quickly taken away. You can become lost, invisible. Trying to re-establish "you" can be an uphill battle, an emotional fight. The person that put you in that position in the first place is going to resist whenever you want to make a positive change in your life. They're going to keep you down and hold you down. You need to make a choice for yourself. Who are you? What's important for you? Who were you were meant to be?

I remember times when my mother would not be allowed to leave the house because my father was afraid she would leave him. Many times, my father would follow my mother around just to see where she was going. Many, many times he would sneak up on her while she was on the telephone. When neighbors would come over to the house and sit in the kitchen and talk, he wanted to know what they were talking about. He would storm into the room and say, "What are you doing? Who are you talking to? Are you talking about me? What's going on?"

It was tough for me, loving and caring so much for my mother and seeing her victimized, seeing her hurt, seeing her beaten and bloodied at the hands of an angry man. I was confused for many years about how women were supposed to be treated, respected, revered, and loved by the men in their lives. They weren't supposed to be torn up and hurt by a man who had committed to them. Seeing firsthand how my father treated my mother, I knew in my gut that it was absolutely wrong.

I remember when I was about thirteen or fourteen, sitting in the kitchen when my father walked in. He was in one of his angry moods. I remember looking at him, and something came over me. Something came through my spirit. I remember looking at him and thinking to myself, *I do not want to be like him*. What a sad, sad thing for a son to think. I knew that the proper way to treat another human being was not the way my father treated all of us. I knew there was a better way. Right then, I made a conscious choice as a young teenage boy that I would take the other road—a higher road, choosing to live my life with dignity, to treat people with respect, as tough as it can be sometimes. I wanted to love and to offer forgiveness, rather than be like my father.

One of the things I loved about my mother, and still do to this day, is that she never quits, and she never gives up. She goes to church regularly. She's always close to a Bible. She prays constantly, and she always loved and protected us kids no matter what. On the other hand, my mother—by today's standards and by some textbook definitions—was very codependent. She also enabled my father, out of fear. That was not a healthy example for us kids.

My mother was codependent because she was not allowed to go back and get an education. So, she depended on my father for her well-being, provision, and esteem. My father withheld those things from her. My father threatened her by saying he'd kick us out on the street or not provide money for our welfare. So, she felt trapped and did the best she could. He had a stronghold on her. But she always kept the faith, always stayed close to God and kept God close to us. It was the faith my mother demonstrated and lived daily that gave us hope and kept us going.

In my memory, my father rarely attended church until later in his life. But, when we were younger, he would "show up" for the occasional Christmas or Easter service. It would always create tremendous controversy, upheaval, and pain. It upset us all. If I weren't a "good boy," I would get pinched or hit by my father right in church. It was my mother who taught us about faith and God and the Bible. She also taught me how to do my multiplication tables and how to read—and she made it fun for me. No matter what happened or how bad things got, my mother loved and took care of us three kids, and she never, ever gave up. She encouraged us, minimized the abuse, confusion, and dysfunction, and demonstrated a consistent faith and love to each of her children.

During the final days of my dad's life, my mother was the ultimate caregiver. It was frustrating for her to not be able to make him well. But, again, she never quit and always showed up for him and for the family. She took him to his appointments and therapies, and she worked hard to meet all his needs. I believe now that she did this out of fear or guilt about not being the good Catholic girl she wanted to be. (She may disagree about that.) But no matter what happened, she was there. She was the consummate, ultimate Catholic and strong, devoted, Christian wife. No matter how bad things got, she hung in there to the very end. I admire her for that. As I said, she was the glue that kept our family together.

Even when my dad was sick and bedridden, he would still verbally abuse my mother—until it stopped.

One day my two sisters and I got together with my mother and said: "Mom, you do realize you're in charge now? He has no power over you. He has no power to take anything away from you anymore. Mom, you can go back and recapture yourself. You can go back and find out who you are. You can go back and you can own your life and not be a victim anymore. Right now, you are free to make your own choices."

But this wasn't an option she was familiar with. She couldn't quite grasp the concept. She had been through too much, for too long.

Chapter 4

My Father's Passing

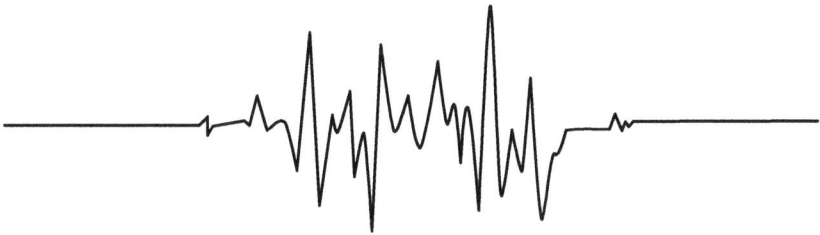

I was at home one very cold day in January when the call came though. I didn't recognize the number, but I knew by the area code that it was from Arizona. I picked up the phone, and the lady on the other end identified herself as my father's hospice nurse in Tucson. She was very professional, very matter-of-fact, and she said: "If you're going to say goodbye to your dad, now is the time for you to come home."

I sat stunned. I had a little coldness and hesitation in my voice when I responded. I was trying to be manly and professional—to be the son that I was expected to be. I knew this day was coming, in which I would take on the role and responsibilities of taking care of my family—especially my mother.

There's a big difference between receiving this phone call from an emotional member of your family and receiving the call from the hospice nurse. She said, "Your father may not last the next twenty-four to forty-eight hours, and it's time for you to come home if you're going to say goodbye."

I scrambled to get tickets for a flight from Atlanta to Tucson. As I drove to the airport, so many things were going through my mind: *How am I going to take care of my mom, make funeral arrangements, take care of my family, and mentally work through the emotional turmoil involved with them?*

I remember getting to the airport and going through security. I finally made it to the gate, and all I wanted to do was get into my seat. My brother-in-law was keeping me abreast of what was going on in Arizona. The hospice nurse had just informed him of the likeliness of my dad's imminent end; he went immediately to the hospital and stayed with my mother and kept me updated by phone, as best he could.

I remember sitting on the airplane and thinking, *Before they close the doors and it's time for us to take off, I'm going to check one more time with my brother-in-law and see how dad's doing, because I really would like to say goodbye to my dad.* I sent my brother-in-law a text, and asked, "How's Poppy doing?" Poppy was a nickname we gave dad years ago that just stuck.

A few minutes later, I got a text message back from my brother-in-law: "We just lost Poppy."

I typed back, "Could you repeat that?"

He answered via the cold cellphone, "Yes, we just lost dad, five minutes ago."

I sat there stunned, a thousand miles away from my mother and my family, knowing my father had left this earth. I don't know what I felt—sadness? Loneliness? An urge to be soldier-like? Brave?

I said a quick prayer, settled into my seat, and felt very lonely. I looked around. I became very aware that no one had stopped moving. The world had not stopped. Everybody kept trying to put bags in the overhead. People kept trying to find their seats. Babies kept on crying. Flight attendants kept trying to get people on the airplane—and yet, my father was gone. That was it. One minute he was here. The next minute he was not. Simply gone.

That flight to Tucson was one of the longest I ever had in my life, and I've had a lot of long, long flights in my career. It was dark, and I felt so alone. I knew I had a job to do—to take care of my family and attend to the task of burying my father.

When I landed in Tucson, my sister picked me up at the airport. We went to my mother's house, where I held her in a tight embrace. We all gathered together that night and, after a lot of tears and lots of somber talk, a little bit of joy came out, a little bit of laughter—and we started telling stories about dad. We talked about all of us growing up and we reminisced about some of the good times and the bad times. There were a lot of bad times.

I wasn't quite sure how I was going to deal with my father's passing. When he was alive, we didn't really see eye-to-eye or get along very well. We didn't have the type of relationship a father and a son should have. There was a lot of animosity. There was a lot of anger; at some points, a lot of hate. Yet he was still my dad. I loved him very much, and now I had to bury him: the duty of the eldest son.

The fortunate thing about this—if there's any fortunate part of this at all—is that I had the opportunity a few weeks earlier to sit down and talk to my dad and ask him questions about himself, his life, his anger, and how he grew up. How he became the man that he was. I think that allowed me to have a little bit of peace, a little bit of understanding, a lot of forgiveness, and a lot of patience with what I was about to go through. I cherish those final conversations with my dad. Those were the conversations I wish I had had with my dad years ago. Why did it take me so long to build up the courage to talk?

Chapter 5

The Funeral

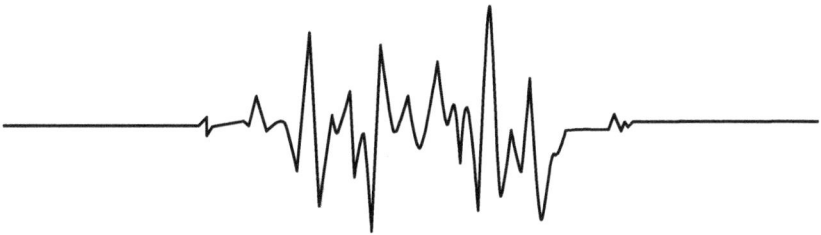

It is both eye opening and somber to walk into a funeral home to make the final arrangements for the burial of your father. It's sobering, and it's final. I'd always had a fear of this day. I didn't know how I'd react to burying my father after all the years of abuse and frustration I'd gone through. It was surreal, but I wanted to get through it, get it done, and get over it.

As his son, I would give the eulogy. It was tough for me because I didn't know exactly what to say or how to say it. But I knew I wanted to say one thing: Goodbye. I wanted to honor my father for the fact that he was my dad, regardless of how he showed up in my life. He was my father. He brought me into this world to learn whatever it was I was supposed to learn, and—good, bad, or indifferent—I'd honor him for that. He had taught me a lot of valuable lessons.

My father used to make fun of me because I could never

hold a flashlight properly. The night before his funeral we had a drain clog in the kitchen sink. It added to an already stressful day. Luckily, one of my family members had a friend who was a plumber. We had to find a flashlight so he could fix the clog under the sink. While sitting on the floor, holding the flashlight for this young man fixing the drain, I had an epiphany. I saw it all at once: my eulogy. I thought, *Dad, you always used to complain and say to mom, "Annette, this boy doesn't know how to hold this damn flashlight." Dad, guess what? Last night, I held a flashlight properly. Thank you for what you taught me.*

On the day of the funeral, I sat there looking at the casket wondering what else I was going to say. I really didn't know until about an hour or so before the funeral. I stood up, looked at the casket, looked at the few notes that I had, and I said something to the effect of, "Dad, you know it hasn't always been great. It hasn't always been good. But I love you and I appreciate your bringing me into this world and for the lessons I've learned."

I kept it light and respectful, and it is something I'm grateful that I had the courage to do.

All I wanted to do at the funeral was support my mother. I remember I didn't cry at all that day. My dad was retired military and he was buried with full honors. I remember the Air Force Honor Guard coming out and picking up the casket with the American flag draped over it. I remember hearing "Taps." The music moved me, likely because of my own affiliation with the military, and the finality of the goodbye.

I walked up to the casket for the last time, kneeled down, and put my hand on it, saying, "Dad, no matter what, I loved you. Be at peace." And I walked away from him for the very last time.

Chapter 6

My Frustrations, My Questions, and a Letter to My Dad

Of the few meaningful conversations I had with my father over the years, one stands out the most in my heart. It was a conversation I had with him just a short time before his death. I sat in his hospital room by his bedside. Before I walked into the room, I stopped and stared at him. He had no clue I was standing there, and what I saw in his face was very compelling. It said so much about the man. He looked lonely, distant, and afraid.

It was very sad to see my father so helpless and incapacitated. Here was a man who had been a vibrant, energetic, "kick butt" type of guy. He had survived World War II and the Vietnam era. He had weathered a lot of disappointments in his life, including the angriness that he grew up with. I saw this man, eighty-nine years of age, lying in bed with his hands over his head, just staring off into space. Not staring at anything in particular, but just looking far off. I looked at him and I had nothing but deep sadness. All the pain and anguish I had experienced because of him seemed to melt away. I went from anger to empathy—a word I never thought I would associate with my dad. I felt terrible disappointment for him because he had lived his life in anger and fear. Going through a lifetime like that seemed so empty and pointless, and now he lay there, at the end of his life, in a sterile hospital bed.

He was very lost toward the end. His skin was scaly and pale and tight when I saw him in the hospital. It was obvious that he was suffering and all that was left of him was a sick and dying man.

For years, my father suffered from lung cancer. He had smoked for more than fifty years, and alcohol was also a huge part of his life. In addition, he was suffering from complications due to respiratory infections. He was now suffering, period. It was sad to watch. His choices had brought him to this point, to this end. It was all about choices.

He needed other people to help clothe and feed him and take care of him. Ironically, the people whom he had hurt with his anger were the same people who helped him in the end, in his greatest time of need. They were the same people who now were choosing to love and support him, clothe and feed him, and sit by his bedside in his final days.

I walked into the hospital room. I quietly rubbed his arm to let him know I was there. I sat down next to him at his bedside. This was my opportunity. Was I going to be angry with him as we talked, or was I going to be the good son and take the lead in having a meaningful, deep conversation? Was I going to succumb to the hate and violence that was so prevalent in my life, or was I going to come from a God-filled place in my heart and talk *to* my dad, not *at* him as he had done to me for so many years? I wanted to talk frankly.

So I asked him, "Dad, I have questions for you and I'd like to sit here in our moments together and just have a father and son talk. There are questions for you that I really would like to know the answers to. Would you be willing to talk with me about that?"

My father, as you've gathered by now, was not a person to talk about his feelings or his inner self. That was taboo. That was something he just didn't do, even now. However, I sensed that he really wished for somebody to talk to him, to clear the air with him and allow him to get things off his chest. I felt that he really wanted to make peace—almost like a confession. As his son, I felt compelled to do the probing and give him the opportunity. I had to find out what was really was going on with my father—who he was, why he was so angry, and why he made all the choices he did.

I sat there and looked at my dad, without any discomfort. I asked him quietly, "Dad, why are you such an angry man?"

My father looked me in the eyes, very quietly and coldly, and said, "I don't know why. I've always been angry." At that point, I got it. He knew in his heart that he was an angry person. He acknowledged it, as well as its grip on him, and I realized that he didn't know how to stop it. He thought anger was just the way that he showed up, and that the anger he had was normal. He remembered being angry ever since he was a little boy.

"Dad, tell me, when did you first see anger, and where did the anger come from?" I pursued the truth now. "Can you tell me that?"

In his short little sentences, he told me that his father was angry—his father used to hit and beat him. He'd go on drinking binges and abandon my father and grandmother, and it left my father angry and sad as a child. He didn't speak very highly of his father. But he did love him. He missed his dad; even though, as a child, he never really got to know him.

That was the key—I hit it! He never really got to know his own father. His father died without ever getting to know his son. I immediately felt sorrow for my dad. I felt sadness for him, a sadness that went deep into my soul, into my being. I realized that he didn't know how to *not* be an angry man because no one had ever called him on it. It was all he ever had ever known.

I asked my father, "Dad, as your son, what advice or insight or guidance would you give me moving forward in my life?"

My dad looked at me and he said, "Jack, never, ever, lie to yourself."

Wow! Am I really hearing this from my father?

Again, he said, "Never, ever, lie to yourself." And, in that moment, I understood his own regret. He had been lying to himself about who he *really* was and maybe how he really wanted to show up in this world. I could imagine it. Living your life as others programmed you to be, not as God wanted you to be or what your heart had hoped you'd be—a person who follows his passion, follows his bliss, follows his voice!

He continued, "Jack, if you have the opportunity to fix something, do it now. Don't wait."

I wanted to ask him more about that. I said, "Dad, are you talking about something like fixing a car or are you talking about a relationship?"

That struck a nerve. He looked at me, and then he turned away with his arm over his head. Then he very quietly said, "A relationship."

I knew in my heart that he had been hurting inside because of the things that he did as an angry man. The way he treated my mother as an angry man and the way he treated his own kids and people around him, both professionally and in his personal life. He just didn't know how to turn the anger off. He didn't know what it was like to be different from the angry man he was. He didn't know how to separate who he was from the anger. In that moment, I saw his deep regret. I saw him acknowledging it all, nearly wishing he could undo it all.

I chose to probe deeper. I looked at my dad, and I said, "Dad, do you remember hitting my mother?"

"No," he said. "I never did that."

I said, "Well, Dad, I remember it." I said it calmly and firmly, so he would understand and not be able to deny it. "Dad, I remember one time, your standing at the top of the stairs, and you had been drinking. You were in one of your fits, in one of your rages, and you were hitting Mom. And at the bottom of the stairs, I was watching you. I was yelling and screaming, trying to get you to stop."

He interrupted the memory, "I don't remember that."

"I do dad," I said calmly, "And you had been drinking."

My father said to me, "Well, if I'd been drinking. I don't remember." His denial was a cop-out, yet there were tears beginning to appear in his eyes. The memories were real. He hid from them in denial. Alcohol had that kind of impact on him, but the choice was still his, and it had hurt us all.

My father went to the grave never admitting to me, or to anyone else, that he hit or hurt my mother. I asked my father during that final conversation, "Dad, have you ever asked God for forgiveness for anything?"

He replied, "Jack, I'm not a religious man. I don't think it would work."

"Dad, it will work," I said. "God accepts you no matter who you are or what you have done. You are a child of God. All you have to do, Dad, is simply ask Him to come into your heart and ask for His forgiveness. You don't have to go out this way."

My father, being a man of very few words at that point in

his life, sat there and just looked at me.

I asked, "Dad, may I pray with you?"

And he said, "I would like that."

I put my hand on my dad's heart. I held his hand with my other hand, and I said the Lord's Prayer with my father. I did the sign of the cross, rubbed him on his chest, and said "Dad, I love you very much. You take care."

And I said goodbye to my father.

***

That's the last time I saw my father alive. I had to know that he understood that he was an angry man. I had to know that he was aware of the pain he had caused. I had to know if he even knew himself—and he did. He just didn't know how to stop the anger.

The sad thing is, I never got to know who my dad really was. He's gone now. Gone. He left this earth and I never got to know who he was as a man—his integrity, his character, what made him tick, and what he would have been like if he wasn't so angry. I was always on the defensive whenever I was around him. He never allowed me to totally embrace and understand who he was. He wasn't willing to come to the table, either, because of his anger. I had to find my own closure, make my own peace. Our final conversation, his acknowledgment, and our prayers together helped in my healing.

Several months following his death, I wrote a letter to my

dad on Father's Day. It took a lot for me to be able to write the letter because of the pain and suffering he had put our family through. However, when all is said and done, he was my dad and I do love him and forgive him, in spite of it all.

Six months later, I went back to Tucson to see my family and spend time with my mother. I went to visit my dad's grave. I stood there at the end of his grave and spoke aloud: "Dad, despite all the anger, the frustration, the alcohol, I really wish I had known you better."

I craved that closeness that was never there. It's sad when a son misses that in his father, when a son is wired to think that his father is an angry person that hurts humanity. It's sad that I never really knew my dad.

Chapter 7

Life Legacy: My Passion and Purpose

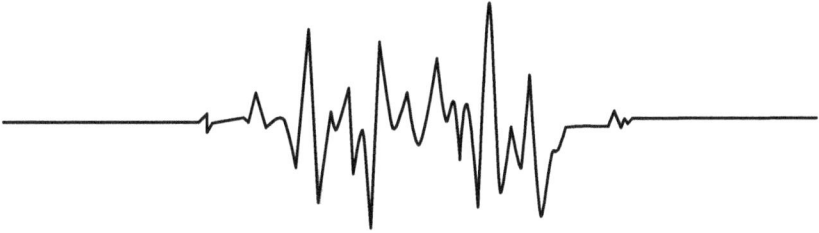

Some people might read this and ask why I would write such a book. Why would I share such personal information and expose my soul?

I share the anger and the abuse I grew up with, and its impact on my family, because no one else has—and I felt it was up to me.

There is so much anger and hatred in our country and our world that people often look at domestic abuse only on the surface. They gloss over it. They conveniently label it to their advantage, compartmentalize it, hide it somewhere, and go on with their lives. And the pain continues.

We live in an angry world. People feel hurt and victimized; and as a result, they get angry. When we get angry, we get stuck in a mode where we want to hurt somebody; we want to lash out physically at other people— at other races, groups, religions, and political affiliations. My purpose, my passion, my speaking about domestic abuse so openly and publicly is because I feel that no child—no little girl or boy—should suffer just because adults can't take care of our unaddressed emotions. When we are angry with ourselves, we project and hurt other people in the process. Children and entire families get caught in the crossfire.

This message must get out to the world, to every person—every adult, child, and teenager. Change has to occur. No one needs to suffer, especially a child, at the hands of another angry human being, nor should they accept or normalize the abuse—absolutely not!

We have a tendency to get mad, to get ticked off, and get angry at other people because we have an inclination to lose ourselves. We lose who we are; we let go of self-control and accountability, and we ignore the discomfort of facing our pain and anger. We forget that we need to show up on this earth. Something happened in our lives that impacted us deeply and we turn this history into anger. We project our own junk and our own infections and our own hurts, wounds, and personal disappointments onto others. The cycle continues and continues through generations. It's a domino effect. Suddenly, everybody is spring-loaded into angry victim mode. We become a hostile society.

It manifests itself in so many ways: by abuse of a child or a spouse, violence in the workplace, or thoughtless explosions of emotion. It presents itself publicly, for example, by walking into a mall and shooting people. People hurt others because they can't manage their anger and have lost themselves along the way. They don't know who they are or how to process their frustrations, so they choose to go out and find ways to release their pain.

We don't have to live in an angry world. We don't have to be the victims of angry parents, angry husbands, angry wives, angry bosses, or toxic friends.

My passion, my mission in life, is to do whatever it takes to spread this message so that people understand: We don't have to live in an angry world. The search for peace within ourselves—trying to truly understand who we are—should never end. I'm determined to share this word in any way I possibly can.

Sadly, I do not have any children. I love kids, but I just have not been blessed with them yet in my life. There was a time when I didn't want to have any kids. I didn't want a child to grow up the way I grew up. I wouldn't want to put a child through those experiences—no way! But then I got older and realized that it's a choice; not all families live the way mine did. I have control over how I talk, how I interact, and how I work with people in my life. I realized that I could do it differently.

So, this is my gift to beautiful young children and to hurting men and women everywhere. This is my message to angry parents: Address your anger. Love yourselves. Love your families. Love your children. Change is possible. Don't live a life of regret. Don't wait until the end to acknowledge your mistakes. Make your peace now.

My passion is to teach others about the impact that we adults have on children. They are always watching us. Kids can see your heart. They can see your soul. Yes, they can! Even when you think they're not watching you or hearing you, they are. They are incredible—open, clean, snow-white books, constantly learning and developing their logical memory. They're developing their minds based on what they observe. What you do (and don't do) imprints on a child's mind. When they see you getting angry, they may perceive it as normal. They learn that it's okay to be mad and upset all the time.

When a child comes to you, interrupts you, and you swat that child, you've just taught them that violence is okay. That's not right. That's absolutely wrong.

Help is available. Begin by forgiving yourself and those who have hurt you. You have to forgive yourself first. Men, in particular, have to learn how to forgive other people. We sometimes think it's not manly to forgive or to tell somebody you care about them. But it is manly, a sign of inner strength. Learning to forgive yourself is the first step. And it's a strong man who can ask for help.

When you're doing something that is not congruent with who you are, basic human kindness is illusive. When something feels wrong and the little voice in the back of your head says, What you're about to do is not right, but you continue to do it out of hate or spite or anger, it's a problem.

A red flag has gone up, and all it takes is for you to back off for a second, pause, clarify the situation, consider the intent, and make a conscious decision about how you're going to respond in a more positive manner.

We don't have to live in anger. We can live at peace with ourselves and the world. In fact, we can decide right now to make peace with our past—and begin to think about our future.

What does your future look like? If you passed away tomorrow and somebody was going to read your eulogy, what would you like them to say about you? What promising words or notes or comments or stories or reflections would you like them to tell?

What would your eulogy be? How would you connect all the dots of your life and turn it into a beautiful painting of yourself?

When you think like that and make a decision about what you want your life to look like, you begin to think differently, show up differently, and live differently. That's what it's like to leave a life legacy.

Chapter 8

Being a Man

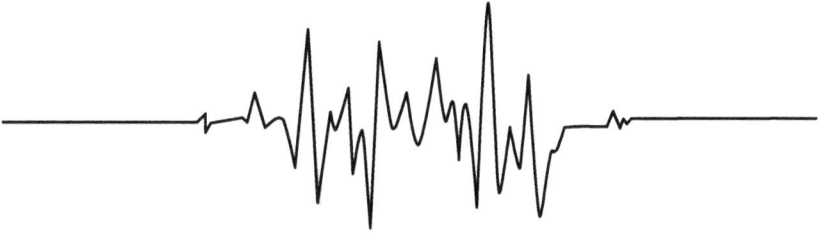

During the many talks I give, I'm often asked about what an angry man looks like in today's world. I talk about how society defines a man's role, how men look at each other's lives, and about our perceptions of what masculinity is. I talk about my frustration when a man doesn't show up as his best, authentic self, especially for his spouse and children. I explore what can define a man and what propels him to be an angry man. Often times, these views are eye opening and revealing to the audience, both men and women.

Anger is not necessarily bad. Anger can be a positive energy for radical change in one's life and in the world. Anger can actually be good, especially if we get angry over issues such as crimes against humanity, crimes against nature, and crimes against the innocent. Justified anger, for example, occurs when you see people that are hurt unnecessarily and nothing's being done to help them. That could be a healthy anger, used to inspire change. (Think of Jesus Christ, Martin Luther King, Gandhi, Mother Teresa.) It's healthy because you are motivated to help people, change the situation, and reduce suffering. It's part of who you are as a human being, part of being one of God's creatures. That is service to others and service to yourself, and it is always for the greater good. It is a positive anger, a righteous anger.

When I finish delivering a talk, it's usually a man who'll come up to me afterward. He'll rock back and forth on his heels and look at me, as if in judgment or self-denial. Often, he's a little bit dismissive of me, as if I'm preaching some pie-in-the-sky philosophy. He'll say, "What you're saying is very good. You're a good speaker, a good orator, and you present your ideas well. But that's not me."

I prompt him to continue. I don't challenge him. He's going to self-reflect as he sees fit. I simply say, "Okay. Good for you. You know who you are. You know what anger looks like and you already know how you show up." I'll just let that accountability go. I know that I have started something deeper. He is churning the information and wrestling internally to justify his emotions, his anger, and his unresolved issues that he has likely justified for a long time—until that moment.

Sometimes he'll come back to me and say, "Let me just tell you a story." He'll tell me a story about getting mad or angry. A story about driving down the highway and somebody cuts him off. He talks about shouting out in frustration, "That son of a bitch! That person shouldn't have done that to me. He should have paid more attention to where he was going. He shouldn't have done that."

I ask him, "What did you do afterwards?"

"Sometimes I just wanted to get on their tail." Or, "I wanted to try and cut them off in traffic." Or, "I just wanted to give them the finger or beep at them because people shouldn't be that ignorant." This is the same person who told me five minutes ago he didn't have an issue with anger.

I quietly look at him. I simply listen and then comment, "Oh, I see. Okay." It eventually sinks in. I often hear stories about, "How my son doesn't listen to me," and, "I just can't get the boy to pay attention to me." I hear their frustration.

We all experience anger at one time or another. But it's when you get mad, upset, or truly frustrated at *all* situations that the anger starts to take over your life. What do you do when you feel anger rise within you? Do you allow it to brew, simmer, and eventually boil over? Does your blood pressure go up? Do you feel that knot of anxiety in your stomach? Do you feel that palpitation in your chest, that surge rushing up your body, and the heat rising? Is it uncontrollable? Do you feel the train wreck coming? You have to choose. You can say, "No! I don't want to do this," or, "I choose not to be angry or not to allow anger to rule or control my life," or, "This behavior does not serve me well. It's destroying everything," or, "How can I stop now and look at this situation differently? How can I respond without anger?"

In our society, we may define a man as a good provider, one who works hard and takes care of his family. He would be a manly man who would come in on a white horse and save the day. A "real man" doesn't cry; he doesn't show weakness in the presence of his wife, kids, friends, and definitely not his buddies. A real man stands up and fights. He never lets someone get the best of him; he takes them down.

Those definitions are old-school thinking: the stereotypical ideas of manliness. We teach it to our kids—our ever-watchful kids. They adopt this macho image and they think they know what being a man is all about. But admit it: that old way of thinking is not valid today.

Society has changed so much. Women are present in a majority of workplaces nowadays. They're CEOs of companies, supervising bosses, in leadership roles. We men have to get a handle on the fact that we may not always be in charge. And, when we're not in charge, we have to keep our emotions and our egos in check. If we don't get a handle on the old thinking about roles and genders, it will continue to be detrimental. We will internalize it until it simmers and erupts.

I can be very stubborn about certain things when I'm dealing with my own anger. I can get so mad sometimes, in spite of my best efforts. For example, several months ago, I had an argument with my GPS. I was driving through the mid-western United States. It was late at night and I was tired. I'd been travelling for three or four days, and I was going to my last presentation. I wanted to get to the hotel in time to get plenty of sleep, so I could be at my best for my audience the next morning. I have a ritual where I like to get up at six o'clock. If I'm in a good hotel, I go to the gym and get a good workout. I get my "sweat on" and start my day refreshed so I can get my mind in the game.

I usually fly from one event to the other. Often, my hotels are a long way from the airport, so I need to rent a car. Accidents or roadblocks or detours can delay my arrival time and I like to be in bed by ten-thirty. I'm incredibly focused. But, the reality is that sometimes travel arrangements have glitches. That's just life. It's how I respond to it that makes all the difference.

This particular trip, I plugged the coordinates of my hotel into my GPS. I have a picture in my mind of how my evening is going to go. I'm going to drive an hour and a half to two hours, go to where I need to be, check into my hotel, etc. It's all perfectly pictured in my mind. Then I'm going to go upstairs, go to bed, and get a good night's sleep, get up, and be the best I can be for my audience with a jumpstart at the gym.

I'm listening to the GPS audio commands, and it tells me what road to go down, what highway to turn on, and where I'm located on the map. "Turn right in 100 feet. Approaching your destination. You have arrived at your destination." I look around thinking, *This isn't my hotel. This GPS does not know what it's talking about. This GPS is full of crap. This GPS doesn't work.* I was tired.

I was getting angry and upset at the GPS. It didn't take me to the right hotel. I drove another three or four hundred yards down the road and still couldn't find the place I was looking for. I changed directions and drove back a few miles. I went right back to where the GPS told me I was supposed to be. I thought, *My gosh, this is not the way I planned my evening. This is not the way things are supposed to be. I'm supposed to be at my hotel.* My anger was building. Things were not going my way. And I thought, *This is NOT my hotel!*

I calmed myself down—or what I thought was calming myself down—took a couple of deep breaths, reached in my briefcase, and opened up the itinerary, which my company provided. I looked at the address. I confirmed it. Yes, that's the address. All of a sudden, I realized that my company had sent me to a hotel that was different from the one I thought I was going to.

The reality? I *was* where I was supposed to be and the GPS did take me there. In my mind—my view, my perception—I was supposed to be at a different hotel that didn't even exist in that small town. But I was willing to sit there and not back down, not regroup, not look at things differently. Instead, I was willing to argue with my GPS, get my blood pressure up, get my frustration level up, get my anxiety level up, and allow my anger to bubble up because everything wasn't going right *according to my plan.* All I had to do was stop, relax, take a deep breath, and ask myself, *Jack, do you have all the information, and do you have all the facts?*

The truth was, I didn't. I was willing to believe something totally different from reality.

We men can be very stubborn about such things. We can be so stubborn when our backs are against the wall and things are getting out of hand in our lives that we refuse to ask for help because "that's not the way a man is supposed to act." A manly man sucks it up. We face our battles. We do the best we can, and keep on trucking, keep on moving on, never ask for help, never shed a tear. What would people say? "He just might be a weakling."

So, what do we men do? We live with fear. We stuff the fear down. We hide from it by not acknowledging it. We keep it hidden in ourselves. We don't share until it's just a little too late. We men are fearful of looking different, looking less than the macho guy that someone told us we were meant to be. We put on a façade, a fake face that says "All is well." Yet just below the surface is rage, just waiting for the next opportunity or the next unsuspecting person that comes along and doesn't show up the way we "think" they should. *That person will pay the price because he doesn't look and act like me.* Heaven forbid the person who crosses your path be a child or a loved one.

When your back's against the wall, you've run out of options. You don't know what to do because of your pride, your ego, your personal frustration, or your personal emotional hurdles. Your own personal, inadequate truths are stopping you from asking for or accepting help, or showing any sign of weakness.

The disconnection begins.

It's a good time to do some self-reflection. Articulate your definitions of a man. Challenge your definitions of a man. Think about the male role models who come to mind and give you a solid example of what you would define as a man. Are there any traits that resonate with you, good or bad?

How is the way you're "showing up" working for you? Is there anything you'd like to do differently? Is it time for a change?

Being a man could mean being a man of character, being a man of truth, being a man of loyalty, and being a man of integrity. It could mean just being who you are and accepting yourself, owning up to it, and not being afraid to show it to the world—in strength and weakness. And, after taking account, make a decision to change for a healthier, better you.

Being a good man serves the greater good of society. If you aren't the best for yourself, you may not be the best for the people who depend on you, who love and care for you—those people whom you influence and impact and, most likely, love every day. Those same people may be the ones who have to forgive you one day. I saw the sadness in my own dad's face as his life was coming to an end. I could tell looking into his eyes that he wished he had fixed the relationships that slipped by him. Sadly for him, there was no turning back.

Interestingly, when I saw my father lying in that hospital bed, I realized in my heart that my father knew that he was an angry man, and in his heart, he did not want to go out that way. He just did not know how to ask for help. He was never taught that it was acceptable for a real man to do so. It takes courage. It takes strength. It takes humility. It takes a true man. He didn't know how to show vulnerability outwardly. He didn't know how to tell his own son that he loved him. He may have thought it was too late.

That's what anger can do to you. Anger is fear. Anger, if it's not understood, if it's not recognized within ourselves, will destroy the wonderful people around us.

You may think, *I can't deal with myself because I'm having issues, so I'm going to hurt somebody else in the process. I will justify my existence and justify my anger by hurting somebody else. I don't have what you have, so I'm going to take yours away from you. I can't deal with my anger, so I'm going to turn to drugs to escape. I'm going to turn to alcohol, turn to pornography, turn to other habitual behaviors to stuff down my anger, because I don't know how to ask for help. Because, if I ask for help it's a sign of weakness; if I ask for help, I'm being weak. I am a man. I can take care of things on my own. I'm in control.*

That's not being a man. That's being a coward who turns to violence. Being a man is being courageous, being strong and facing danger. It's manly to face your demons, regardless of what they are. A man must show up even for a difficult relationship, for a wounded heart, for a disappointment in life, for someone who personally challenges him, for a failed business venture. A man—a *real* man—shows up and displays his true manliness by asking the right questions, asking for help, confronting the uncomfortable and taking the necessary steps to do the right thing.

Being a man could also mean that you tell somebody who's very important to you that you care, that you love that person—saying, "I forgive you," or, "Please forgive me." Being a man is telling the woman that bore your children, "I apologize for putting my hands on you and hurting you. I'll never do it again" (and meaning it). Being a man could be reaching out your hand to help somebody in need, to expose your feelings and your vulnerabilities, and offering your guidance to a child. That's being a man.

Being a man is not feeling threatened because somebody else—woman or man—gets a promotion over you, and not thinking that, because they got that promotion, you can act out on your anger and ruin their life.

Being a man is being a positive role model to a child. Most importantly, it may mean being a dad.

Being a man is being a positive role model, a mentor, a lover, and a friend. It means spending your best energy and sharing your best self with your best friend and soulmate. It means getting your anger under control, understanding who you are, asking yourself the tough questions: *Who am I? How do I show up in this world? What can I change? What can I do differently or better? What's my purpose in life? What's my mission in life? What do I have influence over to create positive change?*

Being a man is about taking action now to correct situations that are wrong—not waiting until the very end of your life. Are any of your behaviors causing you and others pain? Making the change may take you out of your comfort zone, but choosing to stay in the hurting mode because of fear of the unknown—that's cowardice. It keeps you in a constricted position where you're living less of a life than you were designed to live.

If you know that what you're doing—in your gut, in your intuition, in your heart—is not working for you, why not stop it now? If you know that the way you talk to people at work is detrimental to you, why not stop it now? If you know that the way you talk to your child is detrimental to the way that child is going to grow up and look at the world, why not stop it now? If you know that the way you talk to your wife is hurtful—and that alcohol or addictive behaviors are contributing factors—why not stop it now? If you find yourself hitting your wife or hurting her in front of your children and you know that's wrong—why not stop it now? A man would. A coward wouldn't.

There is no shame in choosing to show up to be a better man, to embrace the life you were meant to have—to love others in healthy, wholesome ways, free of anger, free of regret.

Chapter 9

Doing What Has To Be Done

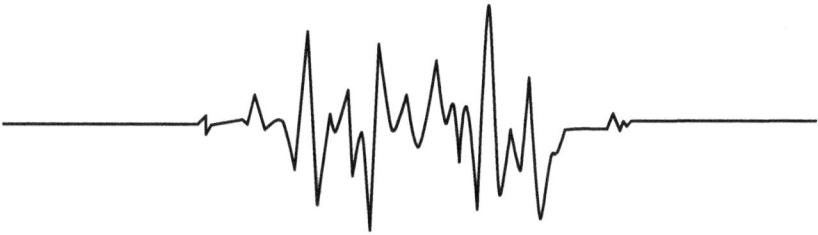

I spent seven years as a police officer in Tucson, Arizona, and I witnessed a lot of horrific acts. I saw so many things that didn't make sense. I saw a lot of anger. I grew up so fast in that period of time.

We used to have a certain swagger and a certain way we talked—a macho police talk. It determined how we got along with each other, how we interacted. When you wore the uniform, it wasn't cool to cry. It wasn't cool to show emotion. It wasn't cool to show weakness. That may have been the real world, but it wasn't part of the job. We had to be stoic and tough.

I remember being on patrol in my police car and getting a call. It was one of the first calls I had as a rookie. A woman had just been sexually assaulted. I was first to arrive on the scene. Admittedly, I was nervous and scared. I had my gun drawn as I walked down the sidewalk of a dark street to the house. I stopped briefly outside to survey what was going on in the house. I could hear the dispatcher talking on the phone to the young lady who had been assaulted. The dispatcher was trying to calm her down, reassuring her that the police had in fact arrived and that I was approaching her front door. I could hear my buddies on the radio and hear their sirens announcing backup was on the way. I mentally prepared myself that I might have to kill the assailant if he was still on the scene. I accepted that responsibility as part of wearing the badge. Walking up to the house I noticed that the door had been kicked in and I announced myself. "Tucson Police!" I yelled. I cautiously walked inside. I saw the young lady standing in a corner of the living room, her clothes ripped apart. It was very obvious that she had gone through violent trauma.

I approached her very carefully and said "Ma'am, you're safe now. I'm a police officer." She turned to me, she saw my badge and my face, and she clung to me. She held onto me with such a death grip, struggling to make sense of all that had just happened to her.

I walked around the apartment with this young girl latched to my body; my gun drawn searching to make sure the offender wasn't still inside. She was unable to let me go. I continued the search room by room, not knowing what I would find, dragging this poor woman with me the entire time. We were quite a sight. I had to stay focused. I had to do my job.

A dozen emotions were racing through my mind. One part of me said I wanted to help this young lady. I had to help and I had to make sure she was safe. The other part of me said I might have to kill this guy if he was still there and became a threat to my safety and hers. I had to fight fear. I stood up as a fearless man. Fortunately, the suspect was not there. He had escaped. But we did finally apprehend him.

The emotional situation was over and done with within two hours. We got her to a safe place. She was in the right hands. I got myself cleaned up. I got back in my police car and I just sat there and reflected, deeply wounded, drained. I thought, *What just happened?* I had done my job. The events were still incomprehensible. I had done my job and now it was time to go back to work. Just like that—next call.

Being a police officer meant doing what had to be done, what I was sworn to do. All of a sudden, I was jolted back to reality as I heard more calls coming in on the radio. I went straight from a traumatic case to something completely different—finding a lost child maybe, or some family not getting along because Uncle Fred won't play nice. Someone was complaining because their garden hose was stolen, and they wanted to file a complaint. The emotional rollercoaster, the constant ups and downs, had to be responded to and endured and assimilated. It could be sustained for a while, but it left you reeling. You didn't know what was going to happen next. It was stressful.

I'll tell you what I did. There was a point as a police

officer where I just sat down and cried. Where did that come from? Was that being a man? What did I learn?

It's cool to cry. It's a human emotion. It's a way of processing all that turmoil, all that stuff that doesn't make sense, without stuffing it down inside. It's being a man.

Something else that doesn't make sense in this world is war. I was a soldier. I was always preparing for war. Being a solider is tough, no doubt about it. Having people shoot at you, being in high-risk situations, going through day-after-day trauma is tough. Being called to give 100 percent in confusing, angry environments will stir the soul of the strongest man. Soldiers are called to do their duty, buck up. Be a man. Do your job. There are times when you have to sit back and take it all in and ask yourself, *What just happened?*

It will manifest itself in different ways. But it shouldn't be stuffed down or denied. Yeah, I've cried. So what? I recall being stationed in Bosnia as a Blackhawk pilot and seeing the atrocities that took place there. We had an area called the "Valley of Death"—so named for the mass graves of the men, women, and children who were lined up, shot to death, and dumped into mass graves. I just couldn't understand or comprehend how a human being could wake up one day and decide, *I will just kill men, women, and children in the name of ideology.* How could someone do that?

Real manliness could also be defined by how well you treat your significant other. Not every marriage or relationship is going to be perfect. There will be good days and bad days, ups and downs. But one thing is for certain: being a man does not involve physical violence or venting your anger against your spouse or your family. Being a man does not mean coming home, having a couple of beers, and demanding sex while your wife is not in the same mood. Just because you are a man does not give you authority or power over her. That's not being a man; that's being a coward.

Being inebriated does not make you a man or give you the right to come home and take out your frustrations on your family. It does not give you the right to change the mood of the entire household just because you're in a lousy state of mind. If it causes your family to need to hide to avoid you, it's wrong. Getting a handle on it, asking for help, taking a pause, taking a deep breath, doing some type of relaxation exercise, finding a safe place to channel your frustrations, or talking to one of your friends is a better alternative. That's being a man.

One of the toughest things men and women have to learn is that you don't have to believe everything you've heard. Mind blowing, isn't it? And you do not have to believe everything you think. We have perceptions and beliefs that we learned in our childhood that we've carried over into adulthood, and we let this become our reality. But the false reality that you have been carrying around all these years can alienate you from the "real you." When you have a false sense of reality, of how the world is supposed to be—and when the world doesn't meet your expectations—your anger, fear, and disbelief will manifest itself in your relationships. Before you know it, you will be alienated from the very people who are supposed to matter the most to you. It's okay to challenge your thinking.

When I speak, I like to do the Blue Shirt exercise. Imagine that sometime, somewhere in your life, someone taught you that anybody who wears a blue shirt is a bad person (substitute your own paradigm if you would like). Somebody taught you at a very early age that you should avoid anyone wearing a blue shirt. Stay away from them. Blue shirts equal nasty, mean people. So as a little boy or girl you learned deep-rooted beliefs about anyone wearing blue shirts. You see this behavior at home. *Blue-shirt people lie, steal, cheat, take stuff from you. They're just basically lazy, bad people.*

You grow up, and you're not quite sure what to do because there are a lot of people at school with blue shirts. Do you interact with them or not? Deep within you is this message that people wearing blue shirts are bad. You are conflicted, uncomfortable, jaded.

Now you have a job. You still have this belief, in the back of your mind. You've had more exposure to people in blue shirts and you should be able to think for yourself, but it's still so unsettling. It's getting increasingly difficult to avoid all these terrible blue-shirt people. It affects everything you do and how you react in every situation. You've based your life on a preconceived belief. You manage everything in your life based upon the belief that you should always avoid the people with blue shirts. It is a negative, exhausting barrier, and an unhealthy belief.

Then you go to work at a company and you meet the HR people. They tell you: "We are glad you're on board, and we're going to take you to your office and show you where you're going to be working. We're glad to have you here for the next twenty five years of your life." Wow, they have a great retirement plan, great medical benefits—all kinds of cool stuff in this great company. You're so excited. You're pumped up and you're thinking, *I'm facing a good career!* They show you to your office and all you see is a sea of people wearing blue shirts. Holy smokes! What do you think is going to happen to you now?

Are your beliefs about blue shirts and what you do with that belief going to hold you back from meaningful relationships and the life you dreamed of living? You go into your new office, bewildered and hesitant.

You remember, "Blue shirts equal bad, terrible people. Don't work with them because they're lazy. They take things." Your blood pressure goes up, your anxiety level goes up, and your heart jumps into your throat because you don't know what to do. You have a few options. You can turn around and walk out. Or you can acknowledge or even challenge that belief and you can choose to stay. Fight or flight.

You say to yourself, *I'm going to gut this out for a while,* and you get assigned to a project with somebody: a very lovely young lady who just happens to wear a blue shirt that day. You're triggered. Then you realize, *This person in the blue shirt is talking to me. This person in the blue shirt asked me how my day is going. This person in the blue shirt just asked me if I needed any help on this particular project. That's weird. She shouldn't be that nice. That's not what I learned.*

Soon, the blue shirt people ask, "Do you want to join us after work for a drink?" You're stunned. You were told not to associate with the blue shirts. You start to realize something's not quite right. Something's stirring inside. Something's different. You feel conflicted. You want to fit in and do a good job, but you've been told that blue shirts were bad. So you step out of your comfort zone and go find out what all this blue shirt stuff is about.

You decide to start interacting with the people with the blue shirts, in spite of your inner thoughts and you say to yourself, *Where on earth did I learn that people with blue shirts are bad people?* You learned it at a very early age. You remember hearing the conversations. Somebody who was influential in your life taught you this. It's how you grew up, how you viewed things. Someone planted those ideas in your head. It could have been your father or your mother. It could have been a best friend. It could have been something you saw on TV. They influenced you. Now you have to ask yourself, *Do I really need to believe that anymore? Is that belief serving me anymore?* And because you're being our new definition of a manly man, you're going to sit there and sincerely challenge those thoughts. Now, you have to step back and decide to take on a new belief. *I choose not to believe everything I think. I choose to believe that not everybody wearing a blue shirt is a bad person. Wow!*

Remarkably, your anxiety and frustration levels come down. You feel better. When you make a conscious choice to change those negative beliefs, you feel different. This is what being a man really is. Being a man is not making excuses about your behavior. It's being a person who says, "I made a mistake. I messed this up. I take full responsibility for my actions. I can do better." And, when appropriate, "I am sorry." A man, regardless of how horrific, how horrendous, or how bad things get, takes responsibility for his actions and does not make excuses for poor behavior.

I learned from some very bright people that we have three brains. We have the logic brain that exists in our prefrontal cortex. This is the executive part of the brain. That's where we make smart, conscious decisions and where our conscience comes from. This logical brain usually starts developing at a very early age. A child is constantly absorbing, taking stuff in, and determining what they believe is their reality. That's the logical brain.

I believe we have a second brain. If you take your index finger and put it in the middle of your chest right above your heart, you'll find your second brain. It's your emotion. That's the place where you feel humanity. You feel caring. You feel love, forgiveness, and tenderness for another human being. That's emotion, that's our heart.

I also believe there's a third brain and that's the brain

right behind your bellybutton. It's in your gut. I like to call it intuition. It's that gut feeling when something isn't quite right, that crazy feeling in the pit of your stomach that makes you uncomfortable. *What am I doing here?* or, *What am I saying?* or, *I shouldn't do that.*

If what you're doing or saying triggers negative uncertainty, then what you're doing or about to do isn't going to be beneficial to you or anybody else.

If you're driving down a single lane road at fifty-five miles an hour, and someone pulls out in front of you and then slows down to forty-five miles an hour you're going to feel some irritation or anger. You're in a hurry to get where you need to go. Those three brains are going to kick in. The logical brain indicates, *That person should not have pulled out in front of me.* Your emotional brain may say, *Man, that was just really stupid.*

When someone cuts us off in traffic, anger is normal. It's what we choose to do with that anger that can cause problems. Do you give the power to the person that just cut you off and let them get you upset, mad, or ticked off? Do you let your blood pressure and your anxiety level go up? Do you want to take the driver out? Or do you pause and ask, *How can I look at this situation differently?* Take a deep breath, relax, and see which brain is kicking in.

There comes a time when everything that you say and do will come back to haunt you. I know that's a pretty rough thing to say. When my father came to the end of his life, there was a point where he saw the end coming, and he wanted to change. He didn't want to die as an angry man. I could see it in his eyes. I could see it in his face and his gestures, and I heard it when we talked to each other in those final moments we had together.

If your behavior is not congruent with what is good and right, the three brains will indicate what you're doing—either in your head, in your heart, or in your gut, or maybe all three. You'll think, How am I interpreting this? How am I interacting with these people? Is it serving me as a person, as a child of God, as someone who works with other people?

If we recognize that imbalance, then why don't we, collectively, stop it? Dysfunctional anger becomes infectious; it gets worse and worse until we finally man up and say to ourselves, *I can't live like this anymore*, and choose to get help. I choose to talk to somebody about my issues and my concerns and about my life. I need to get a handle on how I speak to other people. I've got to get a handle on how I interact and talk to my wife. I've got to get a handle on how I work with the people who are important to me. I've got to make a change to be an effective leader. I choose to be a positive role model in our society and in our world. It is a choice.

We all have the opportunity to make changes today. We can make changes in how we show up, how we affect and interact with our families, our communities, and our society. We can be there as role models. We can be there as mentors for the kids who are trying to figure out their own definitions of what being a man is. And we can be there for those struggling with their own issues.

We can be the change.

Chapter 10

Leading Others

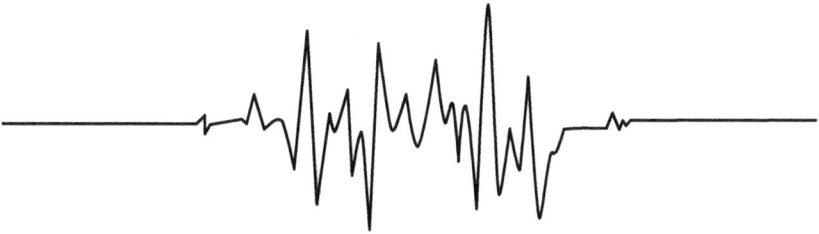

You can read all the books on the subject. You can go to every seminar. You can take numerous classes. You can memorize the latest techniques, get on the human resources bandwagon, know the latest trends, procedures, and holistic thought processes. You can watch other people and listen to speeches. You can do whatever it takes to be an effective leader. That's all well and good. However, you can't be a great leader if you don't take the time and the opportunity to know who you are from the inside out. I believe it's one of the biggest problems in management and executive leadership today—knowing who you really are and looking inside yourself. Doing the hard stuff.

No amount of learning, no amount of reading, can make you a better leader if you don't use your courage to know who you are as a man or woman, as a human being, as a person on the face of this earth. If you don't understand who you are from the inside out, it will be very difficult to put those great teachings into practice.

One thing to remember is that your employees are always watching you. If you are a leader, a manager, a CEO, someone who is in charge at work, you're always being watched whether you realize it or not. If you're angry and upset when you come to work—maybe something negative happened at home, there was a disagreement with your spouse, or you got upset driving to work—you bring that negative energy in with you. Your staff won't understand the details, won't know what happened to you, won't know the issues, and they won't care. They just know you're angry and unpleasant. We may have a tendency, at times, to bring outside issues into the workplace. But remember: an organization or team will take on the personality and behaviors of whoever leads them. If you're a leader and don't know how to get a handle on your emotional responses before you act, before you know it, you are fired or your employees are leaving for greener pastures.

When you bring outside influences and problem emotions such as anger into the workplace, it can also make you closed off to new ideas or new ways of doing things. You won't be open to comments, criticisms, or feedback, which every leader needs to have.

A sign of a great leader is someone who can sit back, look at himself, and ask, Where did I learn to think like this? *Where did I learn this behavior? What is causing me to have a problem right now? Why am I not getting all the information I need? Am I wasting energy on anger? How can I do better?*

Have you ever met a leader or worked for a leader or manager who you wanted to avoid? You'll take the stairs versus the elevator, or you'll veer off and away in the parking lot. You'll see him coming down the hallway and you'll dive into another room. You'll do everything you can to minimize contact with that person. It can cause you to be unhelpful, to lose hope, to give "just enough," to disengage.

Are you a leader like that? Chances are you probably don't know if you are. Employees are good at keeping things from you. They put on a really nice face but may never tell you everything you need to know. How do you think it would feel being a leader or the CEO of a company whom everyone dreads having to deal with? At the same time, your employees are updating their resume, their bio, their LinkedIn site, and their Facebook page, looking for another job to get away from you.

Sometimes ego and pride get in our way when we don't want to hear and understand the feedback other people give us, the feedback we need to hear as leaders. You won't receive the information you need to make the right decisions in the company if you have a reputation for being a person who cuts peoples' heads off.

Maybe your demeanor or attitude is setting the mood for everybody else. So, if you're a person who comes from a place of victim thinking or a place of anger, what type of energy are you putting out there and attracting back into your life?

If something has happened to you outside the job, if you're mad or angry or upset and it's carried into the office, you may be attracting that type of behavior in the workplace. Your employees become careful around you. You may think, *That's just the way I am. That's normal. That's the way things are.* But let me tell you something: If that's how you show up, there's a wake-up call coming. When problem-thinking versus solution-thinking is the norm, it won't be long before a large percentage of your team turns over or you hear numerous HR complaints. Do you remember the *Winnie the Pooh* character, Eeyore? He is generally characterized as forever gloomy, always pessimistic, depressing, always going against the flow, nothing ever goes right for him. Can you imagine coming to work every day and working for an Eeyore? Can you imagine having a team full of Eeyores?

Your behavior at work mirrors your behavior at home. Are you an angry parent of a teenager? How much of your child's life are you willing to not know about because they can't approach you? If your son did something wrong or if he's in trouble, will he come to you and say, "Mom, Dad, guess what I did?" "Mom, Dad, I made a mistake. I know you're going to get mad and get upset and get angry and get ticked off at me, but..." Teens who are able to talk openly have developed a great rapport with their parents, and their parents will calmly respond, "Okay. We've got this. We'll work on it together. We'll deal with this as a family."

But flip the coin over. What if the child knows that every

time they come to their mom or dad with a problem, they're going to get demeaned or victimized, violently hurt or put down, or they're going to be told they're not good enough or a bad person or made to feel shameful? What will they do? Negative reactions hurt, whether they're a man or woman, boy or girl. They always hurt. They shut people down. They destroy relationships, even future marriages. If a child thinks at a very early age that your abnormal emotional responses are normal, he or she may adopt that same dysfunctional behavior into their own life. What type of leader do you think they will be when they go into the workplace or school or even sports? What type of parent do you think they may become? What type of spouse with they be?

As a leader, you need to know yourself first. Knowing yourself first is being authentic, being real with people, being truthful to yourself and others, putting yourself out there, being vulnerable, and knowing your emotional triggers. For example: What if you come to work wearing a nice, clean, crisp shirt and you spill coffee on it? Your initial response may be anger. Yes, it's frustrating, even maddening. But ask yourself this question: Is the way you'd automatically respond appropriate, or is there a better way of reacting to this? Don't get mad that you got coffee on your shirt. It's not worth it. If you make a production out of it and emotionally respond from a place of anger, if you let that little coffee stain ruin your whole day, everybody else becomes a victim too. Laugh it off. Get past yourself. As a commander of an aviation unit, I always carried a small book in my uniform. It was called *The Four Agreements*. It's a small, easy-to-read book. I gave myself a fifth agreement. My fifth agreement was that I'd look up to the heavens and say, "God, please don't let me screw anything up," especially if I was sending crews out in multimillion-dollar aircraft on difficult, dangerous missions. I made a habit of looking to the heavens and asking God, "Please God, give me some help. Give me some guidance here. Let me be the true, authentic person that you want me to be and make the right decisions."

One of my greatest fears was to have to write one of those horrible letters home to a recent widow or widower. A letter telling them that I had screwed up and the person's husband, son, wife, or daughter was killed. I always prayed to be my authentic real self and to be true to what I knew in my heart was right. As difficult as some of my decisions were, sometimes making the right decision was the toughest of all.

A good leader is a person who's not wishy-washy in their decisions. You know who you are. You know your purpose. You know your mission in life, and you know in what direction you're going to go. When somebody asks you a question, you can give them a good "yes or no" answer, or you can give them the information they need or help them find the information. That's the sign of a good leader.

Being a good leader also means developing trust. Do you trust yourself? Have you developed enough personal trust within that you trust yourself to make the right decisions, to ask the right questions, to reach out to the people with influence who can help your company be strong and resourceful, who can enrich your company and enrich the employees? Do you trust yourself and have enough confidence in yourself that you put your employees first and depend on them for the success of the company? Do you build good, effective, professional teams, and do you encourage them?

When you trust yourself and you trust others, it will perpetuate throughout an organization and throughout a company. People will notice. Your people will see it, and they will definitely feel it. Know yourself first.

Chapter 11

Don't Be the Last To Know

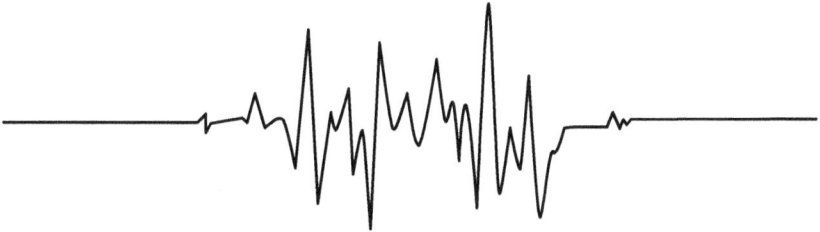

Chances are, if you're the bad guy or the thorn in everyone's side, everybody around you is going to know it, but you will be clueless. You will eventually find out that the reason the company is failing, the people are failing, or the relationship is failing is because you weren't aware of your own self. You weren't aware of the implications of what you were doing. Being the last to know is a very sad place to be.

Let's talk about being the last to know and about self-abandonment. Self-abandonment can come in many different forms. A man or woman can feel abandoned due to the loss of a spouse through death or divorce. Abandonment could be the fact that somebody said, "No, I don't love you." It could be the loss of a friend. You could feel abandoned through loss of a job. You feel as if you've been put out to pasture all by yourself, and there's no one else around. That's a sense of abandonment that leaves you asking, *Why is this happening to me?*

Abandonment can be imprinted in a child's mind if he or she believes that nobody cares. And if nobody cares, why should that child try to achieve? And if nobody cares, will that child tell himself or herself, "I don't matter"?

Sometimes, when we have a sense of abandonment, we feel like we've lost ourselves, we've lost our identity, we have few friends, and there's no place to turn. The worst type of abandonment, in my opinion, is self-abandonment. It's when we give up on ourselves, the Big 'S,' the Self—who we are, who we were meant to be, and how we were meant to show up on this earth. It takes place when we stop believing in, loving, trusting, and taking care of ourselves.

When we feel abandoned, we can be so angry and upset with what's going on around us that we feel like victims. We feel like the world is against us. We feel like we've been set up. We feel like nothing is going in our favor. We feel that the world is like a big, dark cloud that constantly follows us around. No matter how hard we try, we just can't seem to escape it. We feel victimized—*everyone hates me.*

At this point, I feel compelled to put you, the reader, in a safe place. Your feelings of being a victim are simply thoughts, not the reality of the situation. Please read on.

If the victimization mindset becomes who you are and you accept it as your fate, you may begin to feel apathetic about life and your future. Then, because you feel apathetic, you don't feel like doing anything. You just want to sit on your behind, be the victim, and think, *I'm not going to do anything else. Why? Because I'm a victim; there's nothing I can do. The world is against me. Why should I even try?* Or one day you'll get tired of being the victim and then you'll start to go to war. All of a sudden you're always wired and geared for a fight. You get up every morning, take a shower, get dressed, go to work—and you're ready for battle. It's you against the rest of the world.

Usually you'll talk to people like this: "You did this to me. It's not my fault. *You* did that. I can't help it. You're responsible. You're not doing the right things, so my life sucks." Those are the words of a chronic victim. Someone who was abandoned, and worse, may have abandoned himself. Now, he's going to make the rest of the world pay for it.

Victim-thinking can eventually embed itself into the personality of people and even leaders. They've been angry a long time. It affects other areas of life, too. High blood pressure may kick in and all the bad physiological effects that go along with it, including obesity and self-abuse. They're angry at the world. Because they're angry at the world, the results may show up defiantly at work, at home, and at play. When a person is defiant against the rest of the world, they think constantly about conflict; a chronic victim will seek it out because conflict will justify their angry behavior.

Have you ever seen somebody whose mind is constantly looping? They're mad about something and can't let it go. They loop and loop and loop until the issue or concern becomes obsessive. They're looking for the next war. They're looking for the next person "to get." They're looking for the next dispute because, somehow, it justifies their existence in their miserable world. "My life sucks, so I'm going to make your life suck, too." An angry, poor leader is one who is cynical. A poor leader is someone who enjoys making fun of other peoples' lives and misfortunes and exists on pre-judgments and misperceptions. A poor leader is one who lacks character in his personal and professional life. A question I often ask my clients is, "Would you hire you?" I'm surprised sometimes at their responses and, sadly, so are they. The light bulb begins to glow.

Unfortunately, some people in places of leadership are not taught healthy coping skills to deal with anger. Victim-thinking may dominate their minds, and they'll never learn to discover who they really are, their true inner beauty, and their special purpose. Imagine a child who is taught at an early age that he or she is a beautiful, cherished creature. Can you imagine a generation of toddlers who are taught to love, to recognize a person's humanity first before buying into someone else's perceptions and prejudices? "Imagine all the people."

We can see anger everywhere, and it's increasing. We can see it in politics. Turn on the TV twenty-four hours a day, seven days a week, and see all the conflict that takes place. People, groups, countries, churches, and families blaming others for the predicament they are in.

"They did this."

"They're not doing that."

"They didn't vote this way."

"They should have done this."

Just imagine if all the victim-thinking people and naysayers had an epiphany: Cooperation is better than conflict. What if they put their cards on the table from a place of trust, from a place of confidence, a place of knowing who they are as a man or woman? I believe we could alleviate a lot of our daily problems. Unfortunately, ego and pride get in the way of that higher level of consciousness.

Strive to be confident enough in yourself, in your own skin, to say, "It's okay. I'll listen to what you have to say. Maybe I'm wrong. Obviously your opinion is different than mine, so maybe I need to keep my mouth shut and listen to you, because I just might learn something." Wouldn't that be a wonderful place, a wonderful environment? Again, "imagine all the people."

When we talk about taking care of ourselves and understanding who we are, we have to get out of that place of being a chronic victim. Get out of that place of being angry and defiant at the world, and arrive at a personal place of acceptance and peace within. Learn to say to somebody, "I forgive you." Learn to say to somebody, "I would like to listen to you." Learn to say to somebody, "Your opinion is different from mine, but I'm willing to listen to what you have to say." Learn to ask, "Would you be willing to listen to what I have to say?" Come to a mutual agreement, to search for a better way, a higher way, a different way of looking at things. That kind of thinking has the potential to change the world.

What if a mom and dad sat down and said, "I love you and I care about you," to their child? What if they said it to each other? How about sitting down together, putting the difficult cards on the table and sharing a vision? "This is how I see our family. This is how I see the mission of our family. Regardless of how it looks at the end, how about if we talk this out?" Wouldn't that be a beautiful and wonderful thing?

So what gets in the way?

Ego, pride, and, most of all, fear. We just don't know where to start. But not to worry—we just start.

When you get past the ego, pride, and fear issues; when you learn to get past the anger, the conflict, the apathy, and the defiance with the world, that's a great place to be. You finally get sick and tired of all the physiological and psychological effects on you, your family, and everybody else around you. Unfortunately, it often takes something dramatic or traumatic for you to finally get that "aha" moment. It's like a baseball bat hitting you on the head, and you think, *Oh crap! I can't live like this anymore.* You realize that anger is slowly killing you; it's catabolic. You really don't have to live like that anymore.

When we don't know how to get to that place of peace and acceptance and self, our life gets taken over and we may lose control—with sex, drugs, pornography, alcohol, or other addictive behaviors. *I'm not willing to go look in the mirror at myself. I'm going to find something else that's going to fill the void.* Let me tell you, addictive substance behavior does not fill the void. It does not.

One of the neat things about getting to that new place in your life (as I have) is that you learn to look at other people and say to them, "I forgive you." Just like when I sat on the hospital bed the last time I saw my father. The time I rubbed his chest, said the Lord's Prayer, looked him in his eyes, and said, "Dad, I love you and I forgive you." All the pain and suffering I'd gone through in my life with my father just didn't seem to matter anymore. I was able to come to terms with it. It wasn't from a place of victimization, not from a place of abandonment, but from a higher place in my heart—from a place from God. I looked at my dad and said, "Dad, it's cool. I love you, and I forgive you." I believe in my heart that, for a very brief moment when he looked at me for the last time, he got it.

Learning to forgive and learning to tell another human being that you love them is manly. And there are two things we human beings need more than anything else in the world: love and acceptance. When we learn how to love and accept ourselves, we learn to love and accept other people. We can come to a place of peace and inner joy. We can come from a place of compassion and learn how to serve other people. It's good to help somebody. It's good to tithe at church. It's good to assist someone at work who's having a tough time. It's good to tell somebody you care about them, to put your arm around them when they're grieving. It's good to volunteer and help build shelters for people who don't have a place to live. It's good to give money to a homeless person on the street because you come from a higher sense of purpose in your life and not from a place of abandonment. That's being a man.

If you were to talk to a group of soldiers who have been in combat or in harm's way together, you will find that their sense of purpose and worth doesn't come from the mission they're performing. Their sense of worth and purpose comes from the camaraderie, the loyalty, the love, and the acceptance they have for each other and the team. I don't care who you are or what you are or where you are, when you get a group of people together who have faced harm, have gone into combat, have been through stressful missions where they had to depend on each other, they develop a strong, heartfelt, powerful bond with each other. The reason why soldiers fight so hard is not necessarily for the purpose of Mom and Dad and apple pie. They do it for each other—camaraderie, trustworthiness, love, and acceptance. That is being an honorable man.

When you learn to come from a place of compassion, you have peace within yourself. Learn how to accept other people for who they are and not how you think they are supposed to be. Learn to question everything. Learn to ask yourself, *Where did I learn to think like that? Who taught me that this behavior was acceptable?*

When you come from a place of acceptance, you don't take your junk and dump it on other people or start judging them. Acceptance is a very cool place to be. It's like the air being let out of a balloon. The pressure is off. I'm comfortable with who I am. I'm comfortable in my own skin. I don't need to judge you to make myself feel better. I love and accept you for who you are.

When you come from a place of non-judgment, you are able to accept other peoples' beliefs, thoughts, and opinions. Not everything has to be a war. Not everything has to be a conflict.

Chapter 12

Understanding Anger

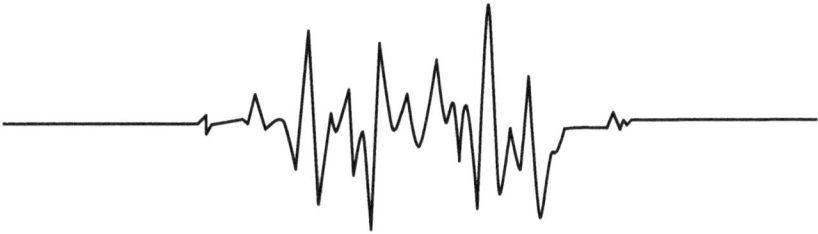

Men tend to express their anger differently than women. We men have a history of being more violent than women when it comes to expressing ourselves. Anger is an emotion similar to love, hate, happiness, delight, and passion. Anger is not necessarily bad. But it is not necessarily a good thing, either. Anger is energy; it is catabolic, negative energy. Anger, when channeled in the right way, can move mountains, change societies, change organizations and the world. We cannot totally eliminate anger from our lives, no more than we can eliminate joy, fear, hate, or passion. Emotion comes from the heart, and we are stubborn and fearful about confronting emotional issues. We will keep them bottled up inside and will not express them openly out of fear of not looking macho, of not being manly.

Angry men may believe that "It's not manly to cry or show weakness in front of family and friends." They have to be tough. Women, on the other hand, are more willing to express themselves emotionally. Though not always the case, emotions make many men feel uncomfortable. I have met men who would rather speak ill of their spouse in front of other men than face their spouse and tell her what is really going on inside. And yes, I have met women that will bottle up their emotional issues and traumas as well.

Men may seek emotional release in other places, such as alcohol, pornography, or drugs; we may have relationships outside of our marriage out of fear of feeling vulnerable to our loved one or intimate partner. We hope the façade of who we really are will stand—better that than to face and admit our failures to the ones we love the most. But the fear will only prolong the inevitable. That is not being a strong man.

It is men with anger issues who seem to be causing most of the problems in our society today. Men will lose their jobs, lose opportunities, lose relationships, and lose the love of those close to them due to anger. Angry men are unable to control and handle normal, day-to-day frustrations like being stuck in traffic, being late, being disagreed with, not having their opinion honored, or not having a child who listens to them.

An angry man is fearful of having his opinion changed. An angry man won't listen to other people. He may feel less than a man because someone else has a different opinion than his and he doesn't want to seem ignorant or insignificant. He may know in his heart what is best for his team, his family, his organization; but, rather than concede, he will stand by his own opinion to the death out of fear of looking weak. In reality, when you have confidence within yourself and know who you are, having your opinion changed would simply be part of life, a sign of maturity and growth. It can be done.

An angry man will insult other people, belittle a child, or abuse a spouse. They will sulk or blame others for their plight, which comes from their believing they are ineffective, unworthy, or unlucky. They may constantly compare themselves to other people. I have met and talked to angry men who feel very hollow inside. They are afraid of ever admitting they have a problem to those who are most important in their lives. They may have feelings of self-abandonment.

These feelings can manifest themselves in so many ways. They may show up in outward expression. Other people can see and sense the anger, though the man does not. Consequently, friends, family, and coworkers will avoid that angry man as a matter of self-preservation and to escape conflict. So, the angry man may feel inadequate and desperate, like a loser, because he can't talk to the people who are most important to him. Angry men usually don't have many friends. They typically don't see that their behavior is pushing people away.

They don't like me. I'll stay angry. Others see it and avoid him. He feels abandoned and the cycle begins again. As you can predict, the anger gets in the way of the man being a good boss, lover, husband, friend, and leader. He's in constant conflict with himself and the world around him.

All it takes is a trigger. An angry man gets his buttons pushed, and in that split second, his whole life can change. When the heat of the moment is over, he may look at himself, at this stranger, and wonder, *Who was that? Who did that? What have I done?* He realizes he has caused damage that cannot be taken back. He will fuel the fire or stuff the pain with alcohol and drugs.

Men, we have to get a handle on our anger, because it's destroying our society. It affects marriages and other deep, interpersonal relationships. The statistics for domestic violence are staggering. The justice system in the United States is bombarded with criminal court cases involving angry men. Eighty-five percent of domestic violence victims are women. When is it going to end? A recent study reported that undisciplined, angry men are more apt to abandon their families and their children than women. Boys who witness domestic violence are twice as likely to abuse their own partners and children when they become adults.

You have a conscious choice. Trust me on this one. You don't have to spend the rest of your life, as my father did, struggling day-to-day to keep it together physically and emotionally. You don't have to go through life hurting the people you work with just because you can't get a handle on yourself out of fear, inner sadness, or self-abandonment.

Getting a sense of awareness and making the choice to get out of an anger mindset is a lifelong process. There are going to be ups and downs, and that's normal. It's having the self-awareness that's absolutely priceless. Setbacks are going to happen. They're going to come and go; but taking positive steps towards this goal, to get a handle on your anger, is the ultimate key and the right track to be on.

I have found myself struggling with anger. I realized I had to make a conscious, tough choice to look at myself differently. I chose to discover new ways to view issues and my own personal struggles. It's a continuous journey of learning. I look for new ways to view the world and how I deal with people in my life—especially those who really matter and who have a significant impact on me, past and present. I learned to challenge my thinking and realized that I don't have to believe everything I think. Being angry does not mean you are a hopeless case. Absolutely not! There is hope for you, I promise you. Anyone can make positive, healthy changes and choices in their life. The most important thing you have to remember is that there is hope. It will move you toward peace and happiness—not only within yourself, but also with others. There *is* hope.

I find that most men don't want to admit they have anger issues, which is interesting, because they will blame others for their feelings of anger. They will blame other people for the way they act: *They aren't doing what they are supposed to be doing. They will need to change and get on the ball before I'll feel better.* When a man blames other people for determining his success or outcomes, he is a dependent man. He is dependent on others to fix things before he can feel better.

Studies have shown that anger and depression may be related. A man may feel anger and lash out at those around him if he feels his life or situation is hopeless. He becomes depressed and may not know how to deal with situations except through anger. Unfortunately, the closest targets of his anger can also become depressed dealing with him, and they may be the ones he needs the most to get him through his darkness.

Sigmund Freud coined the phrase, "Depression is anger turned inward." When a man is feeling anger, he may seek to pass on that hurt to other people, which may lead him to unreasonable actions to stop the hurt. Just look at the news these days: all the school shootings, road rage, domestic violence, men taking the law into their own hands, and even worse, the ever-increasing number of soldiers (male and female) taking their own lives due to lack of effective support systems and their old school thinking about asking for help. Depression may contribute to anger. We may think of depression as a temperament or mood. It is neither. It is a clinical disorder. If a person is feeling low, gloomy, or unhappy, his tolerance level for minor irritations in life will be significantly reduced. His anger response will increase.

No group of people, society, culture, or organization is immune from depression and anger, especially our soldiers. I personally have listened to stories of soldiers who are hurting and angry and depressed, but who will not seek help out of fear of losing their jobs and security clearances, or fear of not looking macho. They live lives of quiet desperation, hoping for a miracle to cure them, a magic drug or help from federal facilities to aid them. When that miracle doesn't happen, a soldier may take his or her own life. These soldiers, unfortunately, may have attached their worth and success in life to a rank or a security clearance or position, which prevents their seeking and getting help. This scenario is more common than you think. It is manly and womanly to ask for help. Please ask for help when you need it.

Have you ever seen a group of people getting along very well? They're all laughing and joking, exchanging banter back and forth, enjoying the moment, and just happy to be with each other. Have you seen a team working together— seen the camaraderie, the positive energy? Enter the angry male or female boss or manager. Notice how the mood and the energy of the group changes. The boss is not happy. He is mad, angry, and upset at something that may have happened during the day, or even something that happened to him in the past. He is holding onto that emotional anchor and doesn't know how to let it go. He is irritable and wants the rest of the world to know how he is feeling. He infects the room with his misery. According to his way of thinking, *You all will pay the price.* Anger is energy, constant negative energy, and it exudes from every emotion, behavior, and habit we've learned. It permeates like a virus to those around us. Others detect it and react to it. If you are someone who constantly projects anger, don't be fooled into thinking others cannot see it or feel it. They will react accordingly out of self-preservation and survival. A boss, supervisor, CEO, or team owner who is angry may unknowingly create a culture of hostility, avoidance, and apathy.

An angry culture such as this has drastic consequences on the success of a company, organization, or team. The angry boss will be spring-loaded to come back with comments such as, "I'm the boss. They had better listen to me." Or, "I don't care how they feel. I'm the boss, and that's the way it is." Angry bosses are fearful bosses. A recent study shows that 70 percent of employees will leave a job not because they don't like it, but because they can't get along with their boss or don't feel valued by him or her.

The "my way or the highway" mentality is old thinking. It's stinking thinking, and in today's world your time as an effective supervisor or boss is limited. You just may not realize it yet. And if you do know it, your anger and frustration level may increase due to feelings of inadequacy and helplessness.

The consequences of anger in the workplace are staggering. Anger in the workplace is an extremely expensive—and very often, invisible—cost of doing business. A 1993 research project by the Chicago-based Safe Workplace Institute discovered that anger and violence in the workplace cost businesses $4.2 billion during the previous year and resulted in 1.8 million days of lost productivity. More current studies place these figures even higher. No matter how you rationalize it, the effect of anger in the workplace is often disturbing, and very few companies are adequately prepared to deal with workplace anger. Some researchers estimate that as much as 42 percent of employee time is spent on trying to resolve conflict. Most experts agree that at least 25 percent of the workforce at any given time is dealing with unresolved, chronic anger issues. Employees ages eighteen to thirty-four are four times more likely to report being angry as those over fifty. One anger management specialist describes the situation as an epidemic of "underground chronic anger."

Anger at home is also costly. Victims of intimate partner violence lost almost eight million days of paid work because of the violence perpetrated against them by current or former husbands, boyfriends, and dates. According to a 2003 study conducted by The Center for Disease Control and Prevention, this loss is the equivalent of more than 32,000 full-time jobs and almost 5.6 million days of household productivity. That's the result of violence.

Chapter 13

Anger at Home

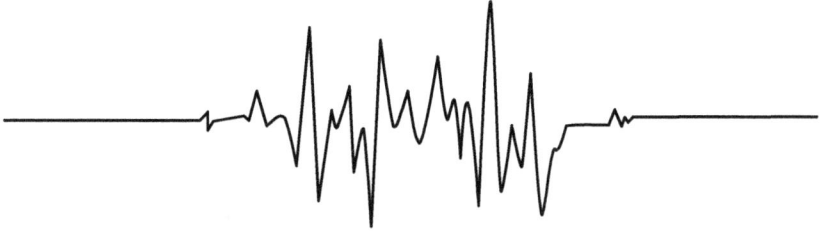

The result of a child witnessing anger in the home can be a long-lasting, devastating impact—not only on the child, but on society. When a child sees their mother or siblings being abused by an angry man, it puzzles them. It baffles the child because they don't know what to consider normal behavior and what is not.

When a child sees a father abuse their mother, it puts anger within that child. The child does not understand why their father would be abusing the woman he married and should love. A child will perceive anger as being a normal way of dealing with day-to-day life. When they have to confront issues in their life, they may automatically go to an anger response because they were programmed to believe that anger is the only way to deal with problems.

Children who grow up with abuse are expected to keep the family violence and abuse a secret. Sometimes they even avoid talking to each other within the family about the abuse. Children from abusive homes may look fine to the outside world, but on the inside they are in terrible, emotional, fearful pain. They may blame themselves for the abuse, thinking if they had not done or said a particular thing (e.g., getting a bad report card, spilling a drink on the carpet, not completing a task to dad's satisfaction, or just breathing and existing), the abuse would not have occurred. They may also become angry with their siblings or their mother for triggering the abuse. They may feel rage, embarrassment, and humiliation. Children living in an abusive, angry family environment often feel isolated and vulnerable. They become fearful and anxious. They are always on guard, always watchful, and always waiting for the next episode to occur. They never know what will trigger the violence; therefore, they never feel safe. They are always worried for themselves, their mother, and their siblings. They may feel worthless and powerless.

Men are very good at holding a shield over what is truly going on inside them. All it takes is that one trigger—that one moment, that one drink, that one extra drug—to push them over the edge. A trigger can sometimes cause them to physically, mentally, and emotionally abuse the people who are most important to them: their family.

All of this confuses a child. It has long-lasting effects. Children are not here to be abused. Children are not born into this world with their pure innocence to be abused by an angry man. That includes physical abuse, but it also means verbal abuse, like being told that they aren't good enough, that they'll never amount to anything. It creates such devastatingly low self-esteem. They become starved for attention, affection, approval, and most of all, love. Their mom may be struggling to survive and may not be available for her children. Because the dad is so angry and obsessed with controlling everyone, he is not emotionally available and present for his children. These children become physically, emotionally, and psychologically abandoned.

Children take abuse to heart. They feel it deep in their hearts. They don't know what's right and what's wrong. No one is teaching them a positive lifestyle. The person who is supposed to love them, to nurture them, and to teach them morals is actually hurting them, saying hurtful things, spewing hate and misinformation. It makes an impression, a false reality, and a lifelong imprint.

It's cowardly for a man to say mean, nasty, hurtful things to a child because that man does not have the guts—the intestinal fortitude—to look himself in the mirror and ask himself, Where did I learn to think like that? *Where did I learn that it was okay for me to abuse a child or abuse my spouse?*

When a little boy or girl sees abuse happening in the family unit, where do they go? They will want to escape and get away. But the one safe place—their home, their supposed haven—is causing them the most pain. Unfortunately, over time, they may perceive that physical abuse is a normal way of dealing with the trials and tribulations of a relationship.

A young man meets a woman, he feels strongly about her, and an intimate relationship is pursued. They begin to share intimate thoughts, spend more and more time together, and possibly marry. One day, a controversial issue presents itself—the loss of a job, a child's grades are not up to par, the dinner wasn't cooked to expectations, the checking account is overdrawn. The man may feel helpless and out of control over the issue, and it becomes a trigger. He reverts to what he believes is a normal way of handling the trigger. And there it is: hurtful words, character assassination of the one he loves. The anger rages and a fist is used. The pain and the memory will last forever; it cannot be taken back.

Violent, abusive outbursts can be passed down from generation to generation. The culture within the family is that it's okay to be nasty, mean, angry, and abusive to your spouse. That's being a man, they say. It's always been done that way.

I say it is not. It's a cowardly way of dealing with conflict and disputes. It's never acceptable or permissible to *ever* abuse or put your hands on a child or spouse. No matter the situation. No excuses.

Children should be taught personal confidence. They shouldn't be taught how to be tough for the world. Toughening a kid up by abusing him, hurting him, verbally injuring him, or putting him down is counter intuitive. When you teach a child personal self-confidence, they can take on the world. They're comfortable in their own skin.

They have learned to view situations in their world and to make honest and impactful decisions in a mature and adult way about situations that confront them. They don't seek to take the low road by turning to physical violence or emotional abuse. And a confident child will stop the pattern of bullying.

When a child is taught personal confidence, they will see the world as their personal playground for success and vision. They will think, *I can accomplish anything*, and they will see the world from a place of self-pride and self-assurance.

It's not rocket science. It's quite simple. Kids need love. They need compassion. They need to be hugged. They need to be told that they are loved. A child needs to know that when they seek the solace of their father or mother, it is a safe place to go. They want to hear their mother or father tell them, "I love you." A child wants to hear that. A child needs to know that their parents support them in every situation. When children have issues or concerns, difficulty in school, or a tough decision to make, they want to go to a place where they know they're safe. That safe place should always be their mother or their father. If they can't go there, they will seek safety or advice from other places, and those aren't always the best places in the world.

Beating, berating, putting a child down is not normal. Men will do that to others when they are afraid to look at themselves. *I will justify my existence by hurting my child or by hurting my spouse. I have that right. I'm not confident in myself. Because I'm not confident, I'm going to take my anger and frustration out on the people closest to me—because I have total control over them physically, emotionally, and monetarily. It gives me power.*

Sadly, some women are in co-dependent relationships. They stay with men who foster violence and anger, who enjoy having monetary and emotional control over them. They may stay for the sake of security or for status. It's still a form of domination and control. It's not a healthy family environment for anyone, especially a child. A co-dependent woman may live her life constantly in fear over what will happen next. *What will he do next? How can I keep the peace in the house?* A woman may lose who she is in life and who God meant her to be out of fear of reprisal by the man she is attached to by marriage or coercion. But she does have a choice.

Everyone, women as well as men, can make a conscious choice to get a handle on their anger and to leave a positive long-lasting life legacy. Learn to say, "I love you." Learn to forgive. Learn to tell the person you've hurt that you're sorry. It is your choice to get your anger under control and to gain control of yourself. Don't let another day go by without doing what matters most to you in life and honoring those who mean the most to you in this world.

Chapter 14

Healthy Choices

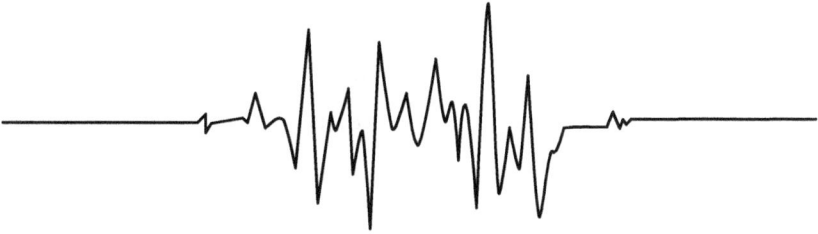

My conscious awareness of my own anger came a few years ago after I lost a wonderful woman whom I was in love with. She decided to break off the relationship. The pain was deeper than anything I had emotionally experienced before. Feelings of anguish and hate ran through my mind to the point where it was almost an obsession. I prayed and hoped that one day she would return and we would be making babies together and creating a happy life. Obviously, this was something that existed in my mind, not hers. I was crushed. I traveled on a nine-hour flight to propose to her. Then, shortly after seeing her, on Valentine's Day, she broke up with me.

In my mind, I was in love and wanted to be married to this woman. I wanted to spend my life with her. I saw great things for our future. Finally, I had found somebody I could give my heart and total dedication to. I do realize, in retrospect, that I could have been a better man to her than I actually was. I believe that it was part of the issue that caused the demise of our relationship. I openly admit that and I own it, but the pain and anger still remained.

I was very angry and upset; it plunged me into a period of deep sadness. I realized that I had to do something with my life. I had a wake-up call. My self-esteem was low and I was not very happy with myself. I had just gone through an emotional trauma and knew I needed to do something.

I've always believed that sometimes you have to get to rock bottom before you're able to look up and get out of the situation you're in. I was taught to be a fighter—to be a warrior, a person who always faces adversities head on. You don't let things get out of control, especially with my background of being a pilot and a police officer. You meet your challenges head-on. And that's what I finally decided to do.

I was sitting in a bar in New Orleans, Louisiana, on September 4, 2007, when I finally said I'd had enough. I was at the bar in a very nice restaurant, looking at a half-full glass of wine. I just kept looking at that glass of wine. Suddenly, I just pushed it aside and said out loud, "No more. No more. I choose not to drink anymore." I haven't had a drink since.

Please understand that, by definition, I was not a classic alcoholic. Some people with a lot of initials behind their name would probably argue with me and say I'm in denial, and that's okay. My job never suffered from alcohol. I was never fired because of alcohol. I never had a DUI. I didn't have an alcohol-related incident. I just chose to stop drinking. I knew that if there was anything I could do right then to move forward and out of that place of sadness, to gain my personal power back, that was it. I realized that I needed to make changes in my life, that I needed to take care of the things that were most important to me—the things that really mattered. I had to take care of the important, valuable things that didn't seem to matter after one or two glasses of wine or a couple of beers. I had a choice: I could let the situation own me or I could own it. I chose to own it. And I did! In my conscious mind I knew that what was happening to me was not healthy and that there was a better path in life, a higher path. I decided to take that new path. I asked for help.

A friend gave me the telephone number of a wonderful life coach, Tracie. My fear and my own paradigms prevented me from calling her for quite a while. I realize, in retrospect, that I was afraid of the future. I was fearful of the pain I would endure making healthy choices in my life. I was afraid of showing up differently. I was afraid of being judged by others. I had fear. But one day, I made that phone call and said, "I need to make some changes in my life. I need help. Here's who I am. Here's what I've gone through."

Looking back on my life now, I know that it was one of the most influential and beneficial phone calls I ever made. I was ready to face my own demons of fear, anger, revenge, and despair. Together, Tracie and I came up with a plan.

I chose not to drink anymore. I realized that the things

I needed to take care of were being muzzled and hidden by alcohol. I was also aware of the history of my father. My father was an alcoholic; if he were here today he would tell you alcohol played a big role in his life up until his last ten years. Then he chose to stop drinking. It was interesting to note that, in my memory, the first time my dad ever openly told me he loved me was after he stopped drinking. I was in my forties, he was already bedridden and nearing the end of his life. I would like to think that there was a healthy correlation.

When I was in my teens, I had an argument with my dad, and my mother stepped in to mediate. Mom asked me "What is the problem with you two?" and I said, "I just want dad to give me a hug and tell me he loves me." He wouldn't do it.

I realize that to get better, sometimes you have to go through a traumatic or dramatic experience in your life. Yes, the crappy stuff. I have also discovered that when you surround yourself with good people who care for and love you, the journey is much easier and more successful. Great people are there to help you get on your way and help you get to a safer and happier place. I was very fortunate to have those people in my life.

I chose at that point to make healthy choices—change my eating habits, go to the gym, change my lifestyle, no more alcohol, and I didn't smoke. I called people I had hurt in the past and told them I loved them. I reconnected with old friends. I got out of my comfort zone. Angry men don't like to be taken out of their comfort zone. It makes them vulnerable. Being vulnerable, I realized, is human. I became more spiritually connected and joined a wonderful church in Tyrone, Georgia—Dogwood Church. And I realized that, to get where I am now, I had to go through some rough times. I was prepared.

I realized that some people have a hard time saying no to addictive behaviors. I know there are people out there whose addictive behaviors have overtaken and destroyed their lives. I wanted to help those people and get this message out to them. Addictive behaviors can present themselves in many different forms. For me, it was constantly thinking of bad things and worrying all the time. It was like I was waiting for the next shoe to drop, the next axe to grind, the next piece of drama to come into my life, the next worst thing to show up, because I had been wired that way ever since I was a child. *Something horrible is going to happen when Dad comes home.* When I was a police officer, I always played scenarios in my mind of the worst thing that could come from the call I was being dispatched to. *Will I be prepared? Will I be able to make that last-minute, split decision to save someone's life? What if I arrive first on the scene and my backup is miles away? Will I be able to handle what may come? Will I be able to talk to a sixty-seven-year-old man whose wife has just committed suicide?* (True story. Sadly, I wasn't able to.)

Then, being in the military as a Combat Search and Rescue pilot (Medevac guy), I never knew what the next mission was going to be, who or what was going to show up on my aircraft when I touched down in a landing zone. *Is the person going to be alive or dead? Is it a soldier? Is it a child? Is it someone I knew? Will I make the right decisions to save this crew and the life of the person on the stretcher in the back of the aircraft?* My mind, like so many of our soldiers today, was wired for the worst-case scenario. We were trained that way. It's a matter of personal survival and mental toughness.

Unfortunately, if you let such thinking consume you and overtake your everyday life, it will dominate you. You may lose who you really are and who you were meant to be on this earth. We are all meant to be bright, rising stars. Our higher power intended us to be amazing, bright stars. In my world, that higher power is God.

I made a conscious choice to make positive changes in my life and say no to addictive behaviors, including addictive thinking. I chose to change the way I looked at myself and the way I looked at other people, the world, the loss of the woman I loved, my own anger, and other issues and concerns. It was tough for me. I constantly challenged my thinking, my paradigms, and beliefs that I had been holding onto since childhood. These thoughts, beliefs, and views were not serving me as an adult. That male macho madness would kick in every once in a while—*I don't need any help!* But God has a way of getting your attention when you don't pay attention to what's going on around you.

I choose to make intentional, positive choices in my life. I'm not saying I'm perfect. I struggle at times with some of those choices, but I know I'm working toward a better end.

Transforming your life can be done. Making positive, healthy choices—getting in contact with positive, healthy people, checking your ego at the door, getting a handle on your pride, knowing how to say "I love you" and "I care about you," having a personal and professional higher awareness of yourself—is the way to have a fulfilling and happy life. Transformation—transforming from within, finding "you"— is an exciting, creative, scary, good journey.

Having an "aha" moment is when you wake up and truly discover your mission and purpose in life. You finally get sick and tired of being sick and tired, and you decide to make more purposeful and better choices. I have changed. I was one of the most stubborn people you could meet. If someone had talked to me about something called "personal transformation," my typical response would have been, "You're nuts! That's that touchy, feeling stuff, that weird stuff you would see on Oprah." Hey, Oprah got it right!

Finding meaning and purpose in your life through personal transformation is powerful and compelling. Transformation could be reading a story to your child, telling someone you love them, being conscious of your anger and knowing how it affects other people, listening to your spouse, holding their hand, and just being there. Transformation can be getting back into a good, healthy Bible-based church or asking God for help. If you're not a religious person or a close-to-God person, just try it one time and say, "God, I'm hearing all these great things about you, but I have a little bit of doubt. If you're there, can you just throw me something?" You'll be surprised. I was.

Chapter 15

Making a Decision to Leave a Positive Life Legacy

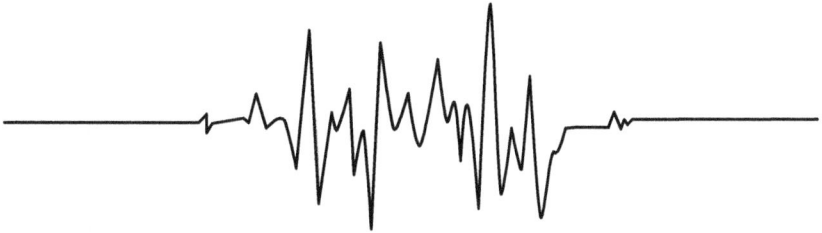

Stepping back and examining your life can be very difficult and very emotional. Look in the mirror with honest intent and ask yourself the tough questions: *Who am I? What is my purpose? What am I all about? Why do I behave the way I do? Why do I believe the things I believe? What is causing me so much pain in my life? What can I do better? Am I happy, and if not, why not? How can I lose this weight?*

I have had to answer these questions myself on a number of occasions and sometimes it resulted in tears. Yeah, get over it; I cry. A traumatic or dramatic event in your life doesn't have to be the impetus for asking these questions. I believe that if men ask these questions of themselves, life will get better. But most men keep silent and stay within their own space. When the realities of their answers come to light within their conscience and spirit, they usually don't want to share the answers with a loved one or a friend out of fear. Some men are able to share. It takes courage. Often, the answers are very powerful and life-changing epiphanies. Maybe the relationship a man is in isn't working, but he doesn't want to have that face-to-face conversation. Maybe going to work every day is painful. Maybe he's not fulfilling his idea of who he wants to be in life. He may want to go back to school and get that degree he has always desired. He may have an addictive behavior that is slowly killing him, but he doesn't know how to stop. So, he continues to live a life of quiet desperation because he doesn't want his family and friends to know that he is not perfect.

We must remember that, in every moment of our lives, we leave an impression upon other people: a coworker, a child, a spouse. The man or woman you met in line while buying your coffee, the motorist you let cut in front of you in busy traffic, the crowd at the sports arena you are attending with your family. Moment to moment, you are leaving impressions upon everyone you meet, intentionally or not. Those impressions can be imprinted upon others based on how you view and see yourself, whether favorably or not.

Remember the people who have left a lasting impression on you? Maybe it was a coach, a teacher, a friend, a fellow soldier, a sports figure, a child, a coworker, your mom or dad. Who are the folks who have influenced you in a positive way?

Imagine that everyone you knew was asked to write a

tribute statement to honor you. They were not allowed to
know where or when the tribute was going to be read. They
were told it was anonymous. They were not allowed to use
the event to condemn or criticize or talk ill of you. They were
only allowed to mention the positive contributions you've
made to humanity, to community, to church, to family, to the
nation, to the betterment of mankind. What do you think
they would say? What would you want them to say? What
would be the lasting memory or the lasting impression you
would leave when you left this earth?

If you're not sure about leaving a lasting positive life
legacy, you can start to develop one now, this very week, this
very hour, this very minute. You can put that drink down, if
it is causing you pain. Talk to a coach or a counselor if there
are issues or emotions that are getting in the way of your
being the best you can be. Call someone you've wronged and
tell them that you're sorry and that you love them no matter
what. Call your healthcare professionals and tell them you
want to develop a healthier lifestyle. Ask people for help.
Join a social club and meet new friends. Join a men's support
group and get involved in the community. Tell your son or
daughter you love them and care for them deeply. Show
them. Tell yourself out loud, "I choose to change my behavior.
I have power and choice over what I think, say, and do, and
no one can take that away from me."

When you leave a lasting positive life legacy, you leave an
imprint on humanity and the people around you. Learning

to leave a lasting, positive life legacy is moving beyond being a victim. It's moving beyond blaming other people for whatever stage of life you are in. Leaving a lasting, positive life legacy is learning to be comfortable in your own skin. Leaving a lasting, positive life legacy is emulating and looking at the people who have made the most positive impact on you.

What if I asked you, "Who are five people you would love to have dinner with?" It could be five people from the future, five people from the present, or five people from the past. What questions would you ask them? What made them so great that you'd want to sit and spend time with them? Who would those people be? Maybe somebody you've already met that has left this life. If he or she came back, what questions would you want to ask that person with the understanding that you would learn from them? Would you implement their answers, their great habits and attributes, and follow their advice to help make life better and make people around you better?

Back up and look at yourself and say, "I choose to find out who I am. I choose to discover who I am as a man. I choose to discover who I am as a parent. I choose to discover who I am as a father. I choose to discover who I am as a leader, as a manager, as a worker. No matter how it's going to look and no matter how painful it may be, I'm going to figure it out and find out who I am." That is being manly, and it takes guts.

One of the greatest gifts you can give yourself in your pursuit of your positive, life legacy is to forgive yourself. Firstly, you need to start looking at yourself and getting past your own limiting beliefs. You need to tell yourself, "I'm okay. I don't have to believe every stupid thought that comes into my mind. I don't have to believe everything I think." What a barnburner that is! Can you understand that? Can you see that you don't have to believe every thought you have?

Some of the greatest leaders in the world—people who have changed our world, who have made such an impact on this earth and this universe—have all been people who have eliminated their limiting beliefs about themselves and about the world around them.

Think about it. Who are the people who have had the greatest impact on our world? Jesus Christ: He got past limiting beliefs. He was a very radical-thinking person. How about Martin Luther King, Jr.? He got past limiting beliefs and changed the world with civil rights for black people. Another radical-thinking person was John F. Kennedy, who said, "We can put a man on the moon within ten years." He was a radical-thinking person and also a man of great honor, wisdom, and lasting influence. Rosa Parks got rid of the limiting belief that black people are supposed to sit in the back of the bus. She was a radical-thinking person as well. Oprah Winfrey is a radical-thinking person who puts humanity first and considers giving back to be the norm. She taught the world the power of uniting for the greater good.

She spoke against the oppression of women and made women aware that they do have a voice.

We can go on. How about Gandhi? A radical-thinking person, he promoted peace and nonviolence in the journey of life. The list is endless. The people who have made great changes in our lives and our world are people who have gotten rid of limiting beliefs within themselves. Look at the impact they've had on society and on our world. Look at the future potential if we just changed for the better: To be limitless radical thinkers.

Think about the Wright Brothers—radical-thinking people. They destroyed limiting beliefs within themselves and within society. How about Joan of Arc? She was a radical-thinking person. People who are willing to look within themselves will discover their true self—the inner core of who they are. It creates happiness. Peace. Tranquility. Passion. The bonus is that, not only can they transform themselves, but they can also make a difference in the world. Changing the world, step by radical step, whether big or small, is an awesome legacy.

Can you just imagine a supervisor, boss, or leader in your workplace that is man or woman enough to sit there and ask themselves, *Who am I? What type of boss or supervisor am I?* As I mentioned before, you can read books all day long. You can attend webinars and seminars and conferences. Unless you know *who you are*, it's going to be difficult to put all that information into practice. The struggle may lead to anxiety,

anxiety may lead to fear, the fear may lead to anger, and the cycle repeats.

When you find your inner peace, your mission and purpose, you're not going to be afraid to show up and admit, "I was wrong. I apologize. Let's take another look at what you have to say. Let's go back and review it. I'm listening. I'm interested."

A person who's not afraid to look at himself or herself and is striving to rid themselves of limiting beliefs is a person who will sit back and ask, *What's another way of doing this besides my way? Have I looked at every avenue? Can I be more encouraging and available? Can I be more empathic and understanding?* A person who gets rid of limiting beliefs will not take his anger into work or make his staff pay for his personal shortcomings.

That takes guts. It takes a lot of guts to be able to do that. I don't care if you're in a political office. I don't care if you're a CEO. I don't care if you're a manager. I don't care if you're a parent. The label doesn't matter. If you're in charge, if you are a leader, if you have influence over a child, a group of people or an organization, you have to be strong enough to sit back, pause, and look at yourself before you can effectively lead. Be the change. Get rid of your preconceived limiting beliefs.

Another roadblock that limits beliefs is assumptions. You make an assumption because something unusual has happened to you in the past. *It's going to happen again, so I'm not going to go forward. Nothing ever changes anyway. I'm just not going to do it.*

We assume that just because something happened to us in the past it's automatically going to happen again. I'm going to stay in my comfort zone. *I'm not going to venture out and try out new challenges in my life. It won't work.*

That's a limiting belief. We assume it's going to fail or hurt us.

Let's talk about interpretation: How do we interpret something? We will interpret a situation in our life based upon how we see the world. You can interpret a situation based upon how you were raised, what experiences you've had. Your interpretation of a situation is your false reality until you ask the right questions. When you're confident within yourself, with who you are, with your position in life, and where you are now—and you have bright hopes for where you're going—it's okay to look at something differently. When we interpret things without knowing the facts and from a negative viewpoint, nine times out of ten we're going to be wrong. It's your belief, your interpretation, your paradigm, but not necessarily the reality of the situation. It's all based on the way you interpret, your special set of glasses, the way you uniquely see the world. Are your glasses the right prescription?

How about the fear of success? That can be a limiting belief. Success can be exciting and frightening at the same time. Have you ever been ready to do something—to try something new and completely outside your comfort zone?

You have the spirit, you have the energy, and you have the motivation. You get ready to move forward and the little voice says, *No, you won't. No, you can't. Stop.* You want to take a leap of faith, but inadequacies and fears prevent that first step.

In some circles, we call that the gremlin voice. It creeps up into your mind and defeats you. But you can beat it. You can get past it and live a very fulfilling and purposeful life. Remember, the world doesn't completely revolve around you. It truly isn't all about you. Get over yourself! Everyone has anxieties and fears. We all fail at times, and then we get up and do it again. The sun doesn't rise and set just on you every single day. Shocker! Find your purposeful life, stand up to your fear, give back to humanity and be the positive person you want to be and were meant to be.

Be comfortable with yourself. Set some goals. Ask yourself, *How do I want to show up in this world? Am I comfortable in my own skin? Who am I?* Don't look at yourself by your job title, rank, position, the color or type of your car, or your wealth and power—but by *who you are.*

Understanding yourself means understanding how you see things in life. It also means having the guts not to dump your junk on other people. Have you ever met people who constantly interrupt? You start talking, you want to open your heart and express yourself, and they immediately want to tell you their story or fill in your sentences or dismiss you as not important. They think they know exactly what you're going to say. But they don't. You never get to the end of your story because they have cut you off and jumped into their own drama. They want to dump their junk on you. Annoying, isn't it?

When I say "don't dump your junk" it means you may have had some fears, interpretations, paradigms, or limiting beliefs within your life. Then you dump those beliefs, for example, onto a child or your spouse. Why would you promise your love and commitment to a woman and then turn around and dump your junk on her? Why would you take a position at an organization or company as a CEO, manager, or leader, and then take all your personal junk that has been holding you back and dump it on other people? How does that serve you? Does it make you feel important?

You can stop. Be more understanding, listen, and seek the truth about yourself and the people around you. Don't make other people suffer with your personal issues, concerns, and problems. Have the guts to stand up and ask yourself, *Who am I? How do I want to show up?*

But how do you get there? How do you get to that place? Write down all of your major goals in life. What do you want? Ask yourself a couple of questions: *Who am I when I'm at my best? When have I been at my best? When have I been at my worst? When have I really felt happy? What did that feel like?*

Write a Mission Statement—I firmly believe this. I have my own. A mission statement is how I choose to show up in the world, my commitments to myself, my commitments to humanity, how I want to serve the community and serve this world It's like having a moral and ethical personal compass. Make following it your mission in life. It can always be modified and changed as you change.

You can take your mission statement (as a good friend of mine did for me) and reduce it down to where it'll fit in your wallet. You can even laminate it. So, when you encounter a situation that doesn't fit you as a person, one that makes you uncomfortable, you can pull out your mission statement, look at it, and say, "No, this situation doesn't serve me." I, personally, will do the moonwalk and get out. I will politely remove myself from that uncomfortable situation and walk away. Having a personal mission statement is very, very powerful.

Major corporations, companies, franchises, most churches, and the military have mission statements. A mission statement gives you direction on where you need to go when nobody else is around. When you're trying to figure out what to do next, you can pull out that mission statement and say, "Everything that I'm going to do is going to support this mission statement."

Wouldn't that be a cool thing to have—your own personal guide, your mission statement? Keep it in your pocket, wallet, or purse and when you encounter people who won't be quiet, when they want to give you their story, when they want to finish your sentences for you, when they want to tell you how you should live your life, when they want to "should" on you all the time, you just politely look at them, stand up straight, and hand them your mission statement. The mission statement may say something like, "I honor myself. I choose to remove myself from situations that don't represent who I am in my heart." Let them look at that. And then you can push their bottom jaw back up, take the mission statement out of their hand, and go on with your life.

Find your peace. I went on a journey. I'm still on a journey. I started that journey a few years ago, and that journey led me to my stronger, more meaningful relationship with myself and with God. This is my story. This is how I now show up. I was at a place in my life that was pitch dark. I was thrown into it when I lost somebody I loved deeply. I had an abusive father who poisoned my childhood paradigm. I needed to change. My first positive step was to quit alcohol. I needed to focus on the new. I knew there were other things in my life that I needed to get a handle on like my physical, emotional, mental, and spiritual well-being. Those are now incredibly important to me.

Mentally, I needed help. So, I found a life coach. Physically, I work with some of the best friends a person could possibly have. My spiritual connection happened when I walked into Dogwood Church in Tyrone, Georgia. I heard a great man speak. His name is Keith Moore, and he is the pastor. I walked into that church at a very low point in my life and I heard him say, "Perfect people aren't allowed." My ears caught that and I said, "I can hang out here. This is where I can be. This is where I want to be."

I developed a very strong personal connection with God, and that is my personal story. I do believe that we all need to try and get to that point. It's where I found my peace.

This is what I want you to grasp when you read this book. There is no more powerful gift that you can give yourself than understanding who you are and asking yourself the tough questions: *What's my purpose in life? What is my mission in life? Why am I here? How do I serve humanity? How do I serve others? What limiting beliefs do I have that have held me back all my life? What gremlins do I have that have stopped me from being successful? Do I think like a victim? How have I looked at a situation and then, when I find out the truth, I realize my whole view of the situation is totally different? What is my passion? What truly makes me happy? What inspires me? What negative behaviors can I leave behind? What hinders me? What traits no longer serve me? What will be said at my eulogy? What would I want them to honestly say?*

Chapter 16

Shout It from the Highest Mountain

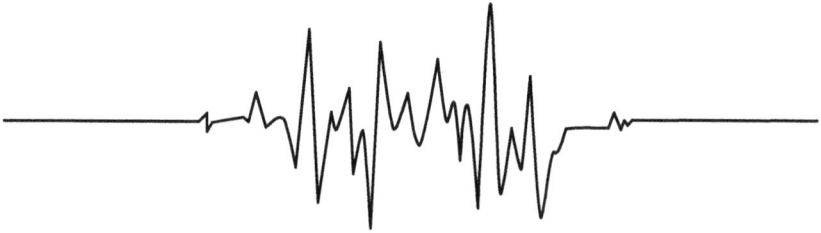

One of the ultimate gifts I gave myself years ago was to not believe what everyone else's beliefs or perceptions were of me. I didn't have to believe what others were saying about me or conform to what others thought. I chose to find my own path and to follow it.

Quieting our inner voice extracts a huge cost. When we stifle our real desires, needs, and spirit—our deepest feelings toward others—we also hide from ourselves. We lose touch with what our true wants, beliefs, ambitions, thoughts, and feelings are—our voice. When we put other people's needs before our own deepest desires, we lose. When we feel a need to please others first before honoring ourselves, we go through life not being completely understood and wasting energy on being someone or something we truly are not. We live a façade. When we choose to live that way, we lose the most important thing we have: ourselves. We lose touch with our deepest desires and needs; we lose touch with our inner spirit. We lose our voice.

I say to you, *shout it from the highest mountain!* Create your message and share it with the world. Find out who you are. Follow your bliss and your inner passion; don't be afraid of what others may think! That is their issue, not yours. Do a self-perception test. (Contact me on my website for more information: www.sourcepointcoaching.com) Go share your voice with a family member and you will be surprised and amazed at the abundance and the positive energy that will come back to you.

Sadly, it's considered acceptable behavior to quiet our real, true selves, especially at work. We are programmed to stifle our real feelings, desires, and aspirations out of fear of reprisal, of being different, of being ridiculed, and of not following the status quo. *I'm not going to say anything, I need my job, let someone else say something.* So, day in and day out, we go through the same routine, praying for something to change to make our lives better. The change may never come, and we live our lives in quiet desperation and in fear of the unknown. This fear, this inner fear that we hold tightly inside, can have long-lasting physical effects on our bodies as well as psychological effects on our minds. We create conditions of illness, sadness, and depression because we are in conflict: who we truly are versus what we truly want to be. We repress our deepest desire, our calling, and our beautiful soul voice. There are mounds and mounds of research that show the direct correlation between stress and obesity. Studies now show the link between stress, obesity, and anger.

People ask me, "How do I find my passion?" It's a good question. Most of us have had a feeling of passion in our life. We just don't exactly know how to identify it anymore. Life and responsibilities have gotten in the way. We grew up and forgot. I think we ask kids what it is they want to be when they grow up so we can get ideas or change our job description. Find that childlike joy. What do you love to do? We may not know how to label it and what it actually means. What would you say if I were to ask you, "If time and money were not an issue in your life, what would you want to do tomorrow morning when you woke up?"

I've had clients who would say, "I want to travel."

I say, "So why aren't you doing it?" And they always have excuses and will throw a roadblock in front of themselves.

I had one lady say to me, "One of these days, I want to travel. I'm very passionate about traveling."

I asked her, "Why?"

She replied, "Because of the energy and because I love to see different people and different cultures."

Then I asked, "What stops you from doing that if you're so passionate about it?"

She said, "I've got family. I've got kids. My husband doesn't understand. We got bills to pay."

I said to her, "You're not passionate about it then." She looked curiously at me. I continued, "Passion is something that overwhelms you, gets deep inside you. No matter what happens, you're going to follow it or pursue it. It's your dream, your energy. It's infectious within you. It's within your soul. It's in your being. It's in your body. It's all consuming and you want to keep moving forward with it."

Passion is when you believe in someone or something and you see the beauty in that person or situation. No matter what happens, you can't think of or do anything else. It overwhelms you. It takes over. It becomes a goal. You're fully awake. Passion is when you see a person who hasn't eaten in days and you feed them, and suddenly everything changes and the veil is lifted. Passion is when you walk up to a small child who doesn't know what it means to love or to be hugged and you embrace that child. You suddenly feel a sense of purpose, a glimmer of change, a burbling of unrest and enthusiasm. And that child finally feels a little change, too, that somebody does care about them, that there is something different out there. It can be as simple as giving back. Passion, great or small, comes in many forms. No experience is wasted. Go for it.

Passion is something you give your energy to, you'd give your life for, and you'd devote everything, even the rest of your life, to do. It's what defines you. You're positively engaged. It's how your life is going to show up. Passion is when you do something and you don't give a damn what other people think, no matter how weird, strange, or unusual it may be. That's passion. It's your inner voice, your joy, and your purpose.

Passion is when you make a sacrifice. You give your best effort. It's so deep inside and so ingrained in you, you can't stop and you can't let go. You sacrifice yourself. You sacrifice your energy. You give tears to it. And when it's over and it's done, it's appreciated. Passion just takes over your life and brings a good, strong, warm tug to your soul. That's passion.

This amazing pursuit can lead you to something that's ultimately fulfilling, something that lifts your spirit and changes how you view the world or that little patch of space that you call home. Remember, it doesn't matter what it is. If it feeds your spirit, and if it feeds who you are—if it totally takes over your mind, body, and spirit and makes you happy—then you know you've found it. And it can always change if it serves awhile. If it serves a purpose in your life, it's passion.

There's no limit when it comes to passion. We all have untapped potential. There's no boundary to it. You feel it or you don't. Passion could be defined as so energizing that you don't want to go to sleep because you want to keep on doing it. You wake up in the morning and you put your feet on the floor, and you go. It's a moment when you look up at the billions of stars at night when you are all alone and you realize you fit somewhere in those stars.

For me, when I found my passion in life, I resolved to live it until my last dying breath. My passion was realizing I had a story to tell. My story would help stop other men and women from hurting other people because of their own personal, warped anger. It would help stop the anger, talk about the anger, and bring it out in the open. It would help find other options to stop the abuse of these beautiful, innocent small boys and girls by their parents or other dysfunctional adults. It would help stop spousal abuse by men who promised to love and protect their wives. All of this has got to stop. If I went through a horrific childhood to get to where I am now, to write this book, to speak in front of large audiences, to make a change, then I say bring it on! I appreciate everything that has happened. I appreciate my dad. I appreciate my family. I love those people who have crossed me and hurt me in my life. I appreciate everything that you've done to me. Thank you for the lessons I've learned, because you brought out my passion in life. Thank you *all* for showing up.

When you find your passion, go do it. Get out of your comfort zone. Get into your un-comfort zone. When you step out of your comfort zone and you want to step back into it, but something inside you compels you—something really deep inside you says, *No, I can't step back. I have to keep moving forward*—that's passion. That's purpose. That's mission. That's taking risks.

I'm proud of you.

All the great thinkers in the world—all the radical-thinking people in the world—have been people who have gotten out of their comfort zone. They got off the couch. They looked in the mirror. They asked themselves the tough questions and came to some pretty radical conclusions: *Who am I? How do I want to show up in this world? What type of legacy do I want to leave behind? What would my eulogy look like?*

I like to tell people that sometimes you've just got to get naked and go dance in the rain. So, go get naked and dance in the rain. I had a client do that one time. She called me on the cell phone and she was laughing and crying. There was a thunderstorm outside. I just wanted to make sure she was safe, but she said, "How can somebody go dance naked in the rain and then go back to the old way of thinking, the old way of living?" You can't do it. Once you get out of that comfort zone and you get in your un-comfort zone, you keep moving forward. That's passion.

Go dance! I'm one of the worst dancers in the world, and I feel very uncomfortable dancing in front of groups of people but I still say *"Dance!"* One of the ways I got out of my comfort zone was to play at a concert.

I finally said, "I don't care what these people think about me. Who cares?" I got up there and it definitely wasn't pretty, but damn it, it sure felt good! Go dance!

Another way of shouting it from the highest mountain is to forgive somebody today—somebody who's crossed you, somebody who's hurt you in the past. Maybe it's somebody who's about to leave this life. Maybe it's somebody who is hurting right now because they really want to talk with you. Take the time. Step out of your comfort zone. Shout from the highest mountain, and go forgive that person. Call them.

Maybe there's somebody out there who needs to be told that you love them. Maybe a son or a daughter needs a hug. Maybe it's an old friend from the past whom you miss or you know misses you. Reach out. Let your soul go. Let your spirit go, and go contact that person. Tell him or her that you remember. Reminisce about the old days.

No matter who you are—no matter how tough, how manly and macho—you can get over stuff, bad uncomfortable stuff. We all want to be loved, and we all want to be accepted for who we are.

There's no more powerful gift you can give a child than unconditional love and acceptance. Men out there: There is no greater gift than to look at the woman who has given you your children, who has committed her life to you, and say, "Honey, I love you unconditionally, and I accept you."

I believe in my heart that there is no greater gift that I could have given my father on his last days on this earth than to sit there in that cold hospital room, rub his chest, and say, "Dad, I love you, and I accept you." I also told my father I forgave him. I gave him my forgiveness. It's powerful, it's humbling, it's difficult, and it's cathartic.

When I talk about getting out of your comfort zone, I'm asking you to try something different. Try something like painting. Go dancing. Go hug somebody. Go tell your child you care about them. Challenge your thoughts. Challenge your beliefs. Be thankful. Do something. Do something radical that will totally blow people's minds, and accept yourself for who you are. Find your message, take that message, and go share it with the world. Shout it from the highest mountain.

Chapter 17

For the Ladies

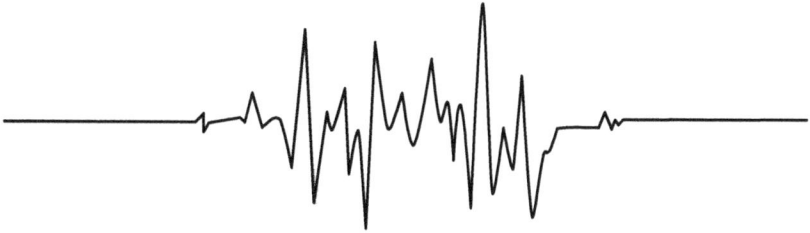

Save yourself. No one deserves to be beaten, hurt, coerced, victimized, or abused—mentally or physically—by an angry man. Never. Regardless of how you rationalize or justify it in your mind, you are not responsible for the anger that resides and is exhibited by an angry man. Period.

He may blame you for his behavior. Many angry men will go through life blaming others for their personal and professional shortcomings, and you are the closest target. You will be the one he blames. A spouse or girlfriend, and even his male friends, can see through the angry man to who he truly is. The rest of us do not know him like you do. He may be living behind a façade. The outside world is clueless. You are the one who knows why he didn't receive that promotion he feels he deserved. He is so charming at dinner parties and you hear him speak delightfully to others, but you know the truth. You know his past and his history. You are a threat to his ego, pride, and vulnerabilities. You may be the first one he hurts to protect his faulted ego, his pride, his insecurities, and his shame. You are not responsible for his behavior. He is a grown man and responsible for how he acts, what he says, and what he does. Not you. When you feel like you're on pins and needles and the day-to-day interactions with him are unpredictable, be careful.

You know you are in a relationship with an angry man. So why are you staying? What keeps you in the relationship? What about your children? If you attach your happiness to his day-to-day moods and behaviors, and you find yourself making excuses or covering for your husband's behavior, chances are you are in a co-dependent relationship. Being co-dependent doesn't make you a bad or pathetic person; it doesn't make you defective or "less than." You may have been scripted or programmed (if I may use that word) at an early age that co-dependent tendencies were normal. You may have seen your mother act the same way and developed a "logic memory" that this behavior was normal, even though some part of you found it odd behavior. Your interpretations of your religion or the society around you may have scripted you to believe that tolerating and reprogramming yourself toward abuse was okay. You may have developed the habit of not telling anyone of the pain you are suffering because it will be embarrassing. The "What Will the Neighbors Say Syndrome." A small voice within you says, *In order for me to survive or protect myself, I must change my behavior to get along.* Chances are, you are in a co-dependent, victimizing relationship, and you know it.

Living a day-to-day life is difficult enough with "normal" people. So why would you want to put up with the extra pain and burden of living with a dysfunctional, angry person whose everyday mission is to defeat and demean the people who love and care for him the most?

Over the years, I have read great literature and reviewed numerous studies on co-dependence and anger. I am also well-versed in finding passion and my own direction in life. I, too, have had to come to grips with my own anger and codependency in relationships. I had to have an "aha" moment, an awakening, and a heightened sense of self-awareness to know that my reactive behavior was unhealthy and could be defined as co-dependent. I had to develop awareness within myself of what was healthy and what was not. I chose to take a hard look at the relationships I was attracting into my life.

A co-dependent person may blame himself or herself for another person's mood or behavior and feel bad about it. A co-dependent person will always try to please other people before trying to please himself or herself. Other traits? "I feel safest when I am giving of myself. I will say yes to a situation when my heart, my gut really means no. I don't stop the situation from continuing (like saying no to a marriage proposal). I find needy people are attracted to me."

And more: "I find needy people very attractive. They provide me with the sensitivity and validation I so desperately need in my life. I feel responsible for other people's success instead of my own. I want to help them achieve personal well-being at the cost of my own. I take on other person's anxiety, shame, and guilt when they have a problem. I try to anticipate other people's needs before my own." These are crucial signs of a potential co-dependent person or relationship.

The term *co-dependency* has been around for almost four decades. Although it originally applied to spouses of alcoholics, first called co-alcoholics, researchers revealed that the characteristics of co-dependents were much more prevalent in the general population than had been imagined. In fact, they found that if you were raised in a dysfunctional family or had an ill parent, you're likely to be codependent.

Here's a story:

Stephanie met her husband in high school. They were star-crossed lovers, and everyone said they belonged together, the perfect, cute couple. Oh, what a perfect life they would have. The script was written and the two beautiful lovers followed the script to a T. Arthur was "The Man." He said and did all the right things to fit into that scripted mold that his classmates and his parents had written for him.

They went off to college, separated for a bit, but eventually got back together. Stephanie was more geared toward the arts and service to others. Arthur fell into the role of being the breadwinner and the achiever. He and Stephanie finished college and, staying with the script, Arthur asked Stephanie to marry him. Oh, what a magical moment it was for one and all, the perfect couple was fulfilling everyone's scripted life dream—a magical time for everyone.

What wasn't obvious was that Arthur had anger issues that he kept very well hidden from Stephanie. After all, it was a perfect marriage, and we all know that perfect marriages and relationships don't have problems. Arthur's anger was scripted to him as a small boy: that all men of color were bad people, and one should not encourage or promote their acceptance in society. No. Such a thing was not acceptable in the family. Arthur, being the expert at living behind a façade, would never outwardly admit to this limiting belief. He knew that showing such hate and discord outwardly was not socially acceptable. This belief would only show itself whenever he felt threatened or challenged by someone of color, and for the most part, his response was measured and subdued.

Except when he was home with his beloved,

perfect spouse. She paid the price. She would hear the rampaging and the hurtful, nasty comments that spewed from his mouth. Stephanie knew in her heart something wasn't right. She made excuses for Arthur's behavior, and comments. Not only did Arthur react to people of color, it manifested into other areas, like his day-to-day frustrations and talking ill of other people. It came through as cynicism, verbal bullying, gossip, and put-downs. A perfect, peaceful, scripted life was marred.

Stephanie still had hopes and dreams of serving mankind and leaving her mark on the world, and she still wanted to have a positive legacy in her life. But she felt stifled, trapped; her heart knew something was wrong. Sadly, she started to buy into what her husband was saying, only to catch her thoughts and think, "No this isn't right." She realized that something in her spirit, in her heart had changed—and she couldn't stop it. She prayed about it and talked to her friends, at least the ones that would listen. Something was burbling deep within her soul.

Arthur and Stephanie were having their first child; it was a magical moment for Stephanie. She dreamed of being a mom, having a good husband, and raising great kids. During that one special moment when their beautiful baby boy was born, everything was perfect. Her first-born child was placed on her breast. The tears flowed for several minutes as she gazed into the eyes of this beautiful baby boy, her son. Arthur was there by her side; she turned to him with their beautiful miracle in her arms, her eyes full of love and joy, and his only response was "That's nice. How much longer do you think you'll have to be here in the hospital?"

At that moment, in that brief defining moment of her life, in that nanosecond she realized she had made a mistake. She had married the wrong man. She didn't know who he was—his true character had just blazed through. She was hoping he would at least share in this wonderful moment that they created together. Her heart sank, but for the next twelve years she stayed married to Arthur.

They had a second, wonderful child, and then that was it. Arthur's anger got worse over time, and the relationship simply became more dysfunctional. But Stephanie didn't know how to escape. She stayed as long as she possibly could until adultery, pornography, and lies became the norm in the relationship. Arthur started to blame others for his mistakes and personal shortcomings. "It is their fault, not mine. I deserved that promotion."

And sadly, Arthur started teaching his two wonderful children all of the false paradigms and beliefs he had of people of color. He infected their minds with false truths that were true only in his world. He perpetuated the cycle of cynicism, hate, and false truths. Stephanie did eventually escape. She went on a journey to find herself and to carry on her mission to serve humanity. She managed to find the wonderful, beautiful person that God intended her to be and to raise two wonderful, beautiful children.

Here's another story:
Susan was in a co-dependent relationship. She gave herself to her husband. He controlled the money; he controlled where she went, whom she was with, and how she did things. He even suggested what to wear so as not to embarrass him when they went out. Her husband controlled everything. He was a sociopath and extremely narcissistic. It was his world and the rest of us were just in it. His demeanor

and behavior even showed up at work in his interactions with other employees, and in social situations.

Susan was left penniless when her husband decided to walk away. She was unprepared, but knew she had to survive. She dated, met several different men, and then developed a profile of the type of man she was going to marry. She didn't want to swim in the deep end, so to speak, of having to take care of herself and rediscover who she was meant to be in this world. "I will go back to what is comfortable, and settle. Life will be good." She was looking for a rescuer; Susan was looking for a man to save her from herself. And she found him. She remarried back into the same situation as before. She is now married to a controlling, manipulating, and dictatorial man and is miserable again. She hides it well as she lives a life of quiet desperation.

I have met so many wonderful and beautiful women who attach their self-worth to the actions (or lack of actions) of a male figure. A father tells his daughter that she will never amount to anything; that she is not good enough for a good man. Sometimes a daughter is sexually abused by her father, only to grow up believing a skewed view of what love should look like. She has a dysfunctional view of what is acceptable behavior. A young woman may have a false paradigm about herself. Due to her feelings of unworthiness, her lack of unconditional love and respect, she usually attracts the wrong man. She misses the importance of a positive male role model in her life. Every daughter desperately wants that connection. She may seek that affection and solitude in the arms of someone who lacks character and who may cause her deep emotional and physical pain.

One of my clients does not like her male partner to be gone more than three to five days at a stretch. She gets anxious and nervous about his absence, and her insecure mind starts to wander. Her emotions get the best of her, and she feels compelled to call and keep track of him. He isn't doing anything wrong, but she can never prove it in her mind. When I inquired about this behavior, she told me a story in which her father walked away from her mother when she was about four years old. One day he just disappeared, never to return. She spent years trying to prove she was worthy of his love and acceptance. Her father had an anger problem. She went on to be a very well-educated and respected professional—yet always in the back of her mind she had that lingering feeling of pending loss of any male figure in her life. She now attaches herself to any strong male who may provide affection or protection for her. She never fully recovered from the loss of that first strong male role model. Whenever she moves for her career, she will break off a relationship if her male counterpart cannot pick up and leave with her. She continuously seeks out that next strong man to take care of her at her next job location.

Never allow a man to convince you that you are less than what God intended you to be. (If you have an issue with the use of the word "God," then define God as you see fit as a "higher power.") One of the most powerful tools a woman has is to ask herself simply, *Who am I?* Not as a statement of a role you play out in life, but by asking a deep honest question of yourself, *Who am I?* Let the thoughts settle in your mind, let your mind wander and stir. You may feel a little sorrow or you may feel joy. Either way, let the thought simmer and flow. See where your mind goes. What did you discover? What thoughts keep coming back into your mind? What visuals did you see? Write them down. Perform this exercise two or three times a day for a week. What is the common theme, the thread? Where did your mind take you? What are you going to do about it? What is your next step? Will you climb that mountain and shout to the world "I AM!"?

If you are in an abusive relationship and you know it, you are ultimately responsible for your own personal safety. Have a plan to escape, set some money aside, tell your friends and close associates, and seek the help of a woman's advocacy group. I can only imagine how tough the decision may be for you to leave, but nobody deserves to be abused, belittled, bullied, or harassed by another human being—especially a mate. You don't deserve it.

Chapter 18

Positive Life Legacy Challenge

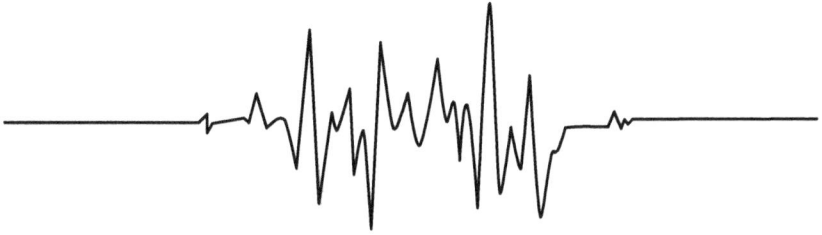

By now your head may be swimming in a sea of new ideas and possibilities for your new life. Change does not always come easy, but change in life is inevitable. Take your time and take a look at what is causing you the most pain in your life right now. Financial issues? Physical, mental, or social issues? Is it your weight? Is it another person? Is it a situation that's causing you a lot of distress, physical or mental? Maybe it's a situation that you want to challenge. A life legacy challenge means facing your issues and realities head on. It is finding ways to deal with them and work through them; healthy ways that don't rely on drugs, pornography, alcohol, or any other habitual emotional behavior.

Anger is not right or wrong. It just is. It's an emotion. What will determine the good or the bad is how you deal with it. There is such a thing as too much anger. Having too much sustained anger has long lasting psychological and physiological effects. And, sadly, you program your mind to stay in the anger loop. Are you always looking for the "fight" that never comes, but you are convinced is there? Too much anger will lead to detrimental things like assault, violence, death, and the loss of someone important to you. I am hoping that I have given you some tools you can use to deal with situations in your life that have been causing you so much pain. I hope you have developed some insight into how to keep your anger in proportion to the circumstances that enticed the anger, and how to neutralize the anger when it wants to explode.

Imagine your eulogy. What would you want to be said out loud? If you wrote your own eulogy, what would you say? A life legacy should also reflect your proudest moments in life. When you write your mission statement or eulogy, would you want to share that with your family and friends? Can you sit down and have a conversation with your loved ones and say, "Here is how I want to show up in the world. Here is how I want to leave a lasting legacy. Would you support me on this?"

Our roles as men are changing in today's society. Women are playing a larger role in the workplace today, and an increasing number are not choosing the traditional role of a stay-at-home mom. So, we men are expected to have more interaction with our children, and possibly even assume the role of the stay-at-home dad. Pretty cool. It's happening regardless of whether you agree or disagree. Roles are changing. Be flexible in your daily life. I am not saying cave in and give up. I'm saying be open to the inevitable fact that change is constant in our world. We can either embrace it or fight it, and we know what constant fighting will do to us. It is how we choose to respond that makes the difference.

It isn't cool to be the person people avoid at parties because your demeanor and personality make it difficult for others to interact with you. Don't hide and be the avoider. Get out of your comfort zone and challenge yourself intellectually and socially. Join groups and be with people you may have shunned or shied away from in the past.

It doesn't have to be dramatic. It could be something you could just share and say, "Here's who I am." You can share with a coworker, a spouse or loved one, or people who are most important your life.

In order to develop a good, lasting legacy, learn how to be confident within yourself. If necessary, find a life coach, a good one. He or she will guide you through the steps. Learn to rely on yourself. Check your heart. It's difficult if you don't have a solid self-worth; if you have a tendency to listen and believe what other people say. You may adopt other people's thoughts and opinions about you, which aren't who you truly are. You may be swayed by their insistence on what is right and what is wrong for you, instead of relying upon what *feels* right.

Learn to believe in yourself. Learn to look at your feelings and trust those feelings. Trust those behaviors. Don't go outside of yourself all of the time to get justification for who you are. Look for it within yourself. Once you do that, you'll be an unstoppable human being. You'll become very powerful. If you've been a victim of other people's behaviors, learn to let those things go. Let the past go. If you've been a victim, face it and confront the issue. Find help if you need help. Confront the concern. It's not going to go away otherwise. Believe me, it will come back to haunt you, and you'll have to learn the lesson again.

I, personally, have a tendency to revert back to my old ways, to go back to bad habits, thought patterns, and unworthiness. I have learned to appreciate and be grateful for what I have. Through some really great coaching, I have learned not to give in to negative energy—I refuse to give it power. Learning how to let go takes the power away. I know it's easier said than done. It tends to be very difficult to put into practice. Over time, it becomes easier and easier and easier. I promise.

Your past experiences will not go away. They may be coloring your present day approach to your daily life. They may be swaying you to believe and do things that you really don't believe. You may be living in other people's expectations instead of living in your own. When you do that, you go through living a life of quiet despair. *I wish. I should have. I could have. I really wish I had done that. I really wish I had told that person I cared about him. I really wish I had told that person I loved her. I really wish I could have told that person, before he left this earth, that he mattered to me.*

A story:

I remember, as a young boy, being in love with a wonderful girl named Audrey. I guess I was about thirteen years old. I had just started to discover how neat girls really were. I was just getting past that awkward stage where boys thought girls were icky.

Audrey, in my mind, was far from icky. Something about her was just beautiful. She had beautiful skin and long brown hair. She was very quiet and had a wonderful confidence about her. All I ever wanted to do was just say hello and have a conversation with her. I was totally infatuated. I would plan my schedule so I could walk past her locker when we changed classes. My heart would start to thump whenever I saw her in the hallway. I would get anxious; and the anxiety was so overwhelming, my palms would sweat. I just simply wanted to say hello to her. I never did, I was afraid. I was so scared that the fear took over and kept me from connecting with her.

Who knows how life would have been for both of us if I had taken that first step? Maybe we would still be in contact with each other. Maybe we would have discovered a long-lasting, deep friendship. I will never know.

My point is: I let an overwhelming fear stop me from doing what was in my heart. I let the fear of rejection, the fear of what my friends might have said, the fear of not knowing what to do if she even talked back to me, stop me from taking the first step. What if? I have always kept that moment in my memory whenever I'm faced with a fear or challenge in my life. What if I didn't take a chance? What if I didn't write this book? What if my fear of what others would think of me stopped me from writing about fear, anxiety, domestic abuse, and anger?

Learn to trust your own judgment, and learn your own decision-making process. Remember the three brains: our logical brain, our emotional brain, and our intuitive brain (i.e., our gut).

Sure, you're going to make mistakes from time to time. We all do that. So does everybody else around you. Nobody's perfect in this world. If you acknowledge your mistakes, you'll find that you'll grow from them—a life lesson to live by. When not all my plans turn out for my benefit, I ask myself, *What did I learn from this? How can I prevent this from happening again? How can I improve on the plan? How can I use this information? How can I use it to become a better person, a better friend to the people around me, and a better son to my mom?*

Start taking responsibility for yourself. Take responsibility for your actions. Take responsibility for household matters. Take responsibility for making your spouse feel loved. Take responsibility for planning your future. Make a storyboard or draw out how you want your life to look. People who have a tendency not to know and trust themselves tend to disregard the details of life and just go through life sleepwalking, believing things will sort themselves out on their own. Stay awake! Remember you can't do it alone. Keep your loved ones close. Have a plan. Think it through.

Taking responsibility forces you to be self-reliant and self-determined. Say to yourself, *Today, I start off with a clean slate.* Develop your own moral code and your own moral conduct. Write a mission statement and practice sticking to it. Remove those vices from your life that don't work for you, the things that aren't helpful to you, the things that don't serve you, your family, or the people you work with. Get rid of those vices. Get rid of toxic friends. Stop smoking! Get a handle on your eating. If you're looking at something on your plate, ask yourself, *Is this healthy for me?* If the answer is no, push it away. Stop abusing alcohol.

We all have lapses in our good habits. We have problems. We all make mistakes, but stay the course. It takes time. The idea that you know what's helpful to you can help you break bad habits. It may take time. It may mean making some major changes in your life and asking for the help, love, and acceptance of some of your closest friends and family members. But you can get through this. You can get past the old habits, the old ways of thinking and doing things. Organize yourself. Organize your world. Immerse yourself in some solitude. Get to the place where you can meditate, where you can sit still for a few minutes, every day. Meditate on positive things, on positive attitudes, and be thankful for the wonderful things in your life. Read great biographies and meditate on them. Give yourself some time and space away from the world. Get away from the TV. Don't be swayed by the media, the reality shows, or obsessed by violent video games. It is all exhausting. Give yourself a break from it all— because if you rely on such stimuli to define who you are, you'll never find out who you *really* are in life. Pay attention to your own behaviors, not other people's gossip, problems, and issues. Take the time to look inside yourself.

Create your own life. Don't let other people create your life for you. Write down all the things you want to accomplish. Write down your bucket list. Write down your major goals with money, people, and in social situations. Ask yourself, *How do I want to get there? How do I want to do this? How do I want to show up?*

When life hits you with problems and misfortunes, it can shape your belief system. It can shape how you view the world and make you think differently. All these issues, concerns, and problems happen to us in life to make us who we are. How we deal with these issues and concerns is the key. When we get hit with a problem, do we sit down and give up? Or do we get up and face the new morning and start again?

When you start looking at your past negative experiences, ask yourself, *What did I gain out of that? What can I learn from it? What is the message?* Don't dwell on your mistakes. Try not to be an Eeyore with a dark cloud over your head all the time. People get tired of that, and you'll drive them away from you. Just remember: There's always something good in every bad experience. There can be a good lesson learned in everything, even the bad stuff. Sometimes it can be hard to find. But we still have to try and look.

Everybody has their blips and their slip-ups in life. Lord knows I've made some terrible mistakes in my life. I have crossed people. I have hurt people, and the only thing I can do is ask for forgiveness and hope that I don't ever do it again. This is part of life. Just recognize the fact that, had it not been for those negative or past experiences, you would not be where you are today: a great human being and beautiful person.

Distinguish yourself and your thoughts from those of other people. Life is pretty easy to get through while on autopilot. It's easy to get up every day and act like a little mouse in a maze. You just blindly go along, searching for that token piece of cheese, doing what everybody else wants.

People tell you that you've got to get good grades. You've got to get married. You've got to have kids. You've got to do this. You've got to do that. At what point will you sit back and say, *Where did I go? What happened to me?* Shoulda, woulda, coulda—don't let that happen to you. Plug in your own GPS and find your joy!

Society has a very covert way of handling us all as misfits or condemning us—calling us losers, imperfect, defective. We have a tendency to want to idolize the rich and famous athletes and celebrities or the people who have been Photoshopped on TV and think that's our reality. But it's not. When we start believing in those things, we start alienating who we are within ourselves. Those people have no place in our personal reality.

Ask yourself questions like *How do I feel about the world around me? What defines me? Do I really want to agree with everything everybody else tells me? Do I really want to agree with all the politicians? Do I really want to agree with all the evangelists and religious leaders on TV? Do I want to be led down a path, or do I want to blaze a path of my own? Is having a career the most important thing to me?*

Find a mentor. Find somebody you look up to. Do a little soul searching. A good mentor or life coach can guide you—a pastor, a minister, a confidant. Let them know the process you're starting to undertake. Let them know that you're trying to make positive changes in your life. Stress that you know it's your journey, and you don't want them to tell you how you're supposed to do it. Just ask them to love, accept, and guide you. Take a look at them as objectively as you can. What seems to ground them, making them who they are? How do they find that? How do they stay true to themselves?

These are all interesting, thought-provoking questions. Get a good support system. Take self-improvement classes. Read. Question everything. Some people will say that you're just being moody or that you'll get over it. Don't let people do that. Don't let them dump their mess on you and take away who you are. Find a good friend—somebody you can trust, somebody you can use as a sounding board. Having an outlet like that will definitely come in handy. Don't be connected to negative energy. Some people always want to put their story on you, tell you what you should be doing, how you should be living your life. And they usually give you lousy misinformation. They already have their own messed up lives, but they have a perfect solution to fix yours.

Sort out a good career path. What is it that feeds you? What feeds your heart? What feeds your passion? Why aren't you doing it? Let go of a need to be accepted and loved by everybody; not everybody is going to love or accept you. Some people are going to think badly of you no matter what you do, and some people are just going to love you in spite of you. You don't need to justify your purpose and your existence in life by the emotions and moods of other people. If you are controllable, there will be people who will want to control you. Avoid them.

As you start to change—losing weight, stopping smoking, stopping drinking, having a more positive relationship with your spouse—realize that some people are going to be jealous. They may be afraid of you because you're showing up differently. That's power. That's a legacy. Some people become overwhelmed when a person changes his usual habits and grows more mature and self-loving.

They won't understand—or want to understand—what you're going through. They'll attempt to undermine your efforts or even sabotage you. I had difficulty with that when I started going through a transformation in my own life. I was showing up differently, and it made some people feel uncomfortable. Some people tried to brush me off. Some people said, "That's strange behavior. That's not very manly. Why did you step away? That's very different. Why on earth would you want to try that? Just go with the flow, Jack. Don't make waves."

I just couldn't do that anymore.

Some people look at positive changes in others—a spouse, a friend, a co-worker, an acquaintance—as a threat to their relationship. Isn't that crazy? Some will want what you have and maybe want to change as well. You become the example. What a cool place to be! You can be a mentor to that person and leave a lasting positive life legacy. If they don't want to get on board with you, if they want to resist you all the time, let them go.

Say, "Thank you for showing up in this world. Thank you for being who you are. I don't need this right now. I love you, and I accept you, but I'm not staying in this rut. Have a nice day."

Thinking positively is nourishing. Thinking positively

builds up your brain. Thinking positively can have a very positive effect on your brain—as if you just ran a marathon. Thinking positively can increase your endorphins, increase the serotonin levels in your body. That sounds pretty amazing. Some people think it's pretty bizarre, but it's true. It will take work, but it can be done.

Try to do something wild, weird, or unusual every single day. Just do something! You don't have to believe every negative thought you think. Get out of your comfort zone. Can you dance in the rain?

I challenge you. Say hello to the next person you see and smile. Step out of your little small world. Pick up the gauntlet. Change your life. Change your choices. Change your behavior. Develop a life legacy. Go out and spread love with arms wide open and learn to accept other people in your life.

As I come to the end of this book, I would just like to say that in spite of it all, I loved my father very dearly. I forgive my father. I know that may sound strange to some people. I think my father had a lot of issues that he was afraid to face. I believe my father, in his own way, was a good man. He just didn't know how to show it. You don't have to wait until the end of your life, as my father did. We do not have to end our lives alone and with regrets.

Godspeed to you all! I wish you the best this world has to offer. Enjoy your new journey!

www.ingramcontent.com/pod-product-compliance
Lightning Source LLC
Chambersburg PA
CBHW060051100426
42742CB00014B/2781